RANDOM HOUSE

SPOTLIGHT

ON

Literature

Collection 5

by Burton Goodman

Project Editor: Marge M. Kennedy
Art Director: Walter Norfleet
Production Supervisor: Debra McAteer
Design and Illustration: Educational
  Graphics, Inc.
Cover Design: Lawrence Daniels and
  Friends, Inc.

International Standard Book Number:
  0-394-04287-5

Manufactured in The United States of America.

Acknowledgments

Grateful acknowledgment is made to the following authors, agents, and publishers for permission to reprint these copyrighted materials:

"The Most Dangerous Game" by Richard Connell. Copyright 1924 by Richard Connell. Copyright renewed 1952 by Louise Fox Connell. Reprinted with special permission to use this adapted version of "The Most Dangerous Game" given by Louise Fox Connell. This version can not be used unless written permission is given by Brandt & Brandt Literary Agents, Inc.

"The Stove" from ANGEL'S SHOES by Marjorie L. C. Pickthall. Reprinted by permission of Hodder & Stoughton, Ltd., Toronto, Ontario, Canada.

"Stopping by Woods on a Snowy Evening" from THE POETRY OF ROBERT FROST, edited by Edward Connery Lathem. Copyright 1916, 1923, 1930, 1939, © 1969 by Holt, Rinehart and Winston, Inc. Copyright 1936, 1940, 1944, 1951, © 1958 by Robert Frost. Copyright © 1964, 1967, 1968, 1970 by Leslie Frost Ballantine. Reprinted by permission of Holt, Rinehart and Winston, Inc.

"Antaeus" by Borden Deal. Copyright © 1961 by Southern Methodist University Press. Used by permission of The Borden Deal Family Trust (Borden Deal, Trustee).

Selections from ANNE FRANK: THE DIARY OF A YOUNG GIRL. Copyright 1952 by Otto H. Frank. Reprinted by permission of Doubleday & Company, Inc.

"Home" from THE WORLD OF GWENDOLYN BROOKS by Gwendolyn Brooks. Copyright 1953 by Gwendolyn Brooks Blakely. Reprinted by permission of Harper & Row, Publishers, Inc.

"Dreams" from THE DREAM KEEPER AND OTHER POEMS by Langston Hughes. Copyright 1932 by Alfred A. Knopf, Inc. and renewed 1960 by Langston Hughes. Reprinted by permission of Alfred A. Knopf, Inc.

"Harlem" from THE PANTHER AND THE LASH: POEMS OF OUR TIMES by Langston Hughes. Copyright 1951 by Langston Hughes. Reprinted by permission of Alfred A. Knopf, Inc.

"A Day's Wait" adapted by permission of Charles Scribner's Sons from WINNER TAKES NOTHING by Ernest Hemingway. Copyright 1933 by Charles Scribner's Sons; copyright © renewed 1961 by Mary Hemingway.

"An Appointment in Samarra" from SHEPPEY by W. Somerset Maugham. Reprinted by permission of Doubleday & Company, Inc. and the Estate of W. Somerset Maugham and William Heineman Limited.

The following stories included in this book have been adapted by Burton Goodman: "The Most Dangerous Game," "The Stove," "Antaeus," "A Day's Wait," "The Story of an Hour," and "An Occurrence at Owl Creek Bridge."

90123VH54321

Table of Contents

On The Run

*What is the use of running
when you are on the wrong
road?*

—John Ray

The Most Dangerous Game

(Part 1)

Richard Connell

"The world is made up of two clas-
ses—the hunters and the hunted.
Luckily, you and I are the hunters,"
said Rainsford.

"Off there to the right—somewhere—is a large island," said Whitney. "It's rather a mystery—"

"What island is it?" Rainsford
asked.

"The old maps call it 'Ship Trap Island,'" Whitney answered. "A funny
name, isn't it? Sailors have a strange
fear of the place. I don't know why.
Some superstition—"

"I can't see it," said Rainsford.

The night pressed its thick, warm
blackness in upon the boat.

"You have good eyes," said Whitney,
with a laugh. "I've seen you pick off a
moose at four hundred yards. But
even you can't see four hundred yards
through a moonless night."

"Nor four yards," said Rainsford.
"It's like a wet, dark blanket."

"It will be light enough in Rio,"
promised Whitney. "We should make
it in a few days. I hope the jaguar
guns have arrived. We should have
some good hunting up the Amazon.
Great sport, hunting."

"The best sport in the world,"
agreed Rainsford.

"For the hunter," added Whitney.
"Not for the jaguar."

"Don't talk nonsense, Whitney,"
said Rainsford. "You're a big-game
hunter. Who cares how a jaguar
feels?"

"Perhaps the jaguar does," said
Whitney.

"Bah! They've no understanding."

"Even so," answered Whitney, "I think they understand one thing—fear. The fear of pain and the fear of death."

Rainsford laughed. "This hot weather is making you soft, Whitney. The world is made up of two classes—the hunters and the hunted. Luckily, you and I are the hunters. By the way, do you think we've passed that island yet?"

"I can't tell in the dark. I hope so," said Whitney. "The place has a bad reputation. Didn't you notice the crew seemed a bit jumpy today?"

"They were a bit strange," answered Rainsford.

"Even tough old Captain Neilson," said Whitney, "had a look I never saw before. This place has an evil name among sailors. Don't you feel anything? You mustn't laugh when I tell you this, Rainsford. But I did feel something like a sudden chill."

"Pure imagination," laughed Rainsford.

"Maybe. Anyhow, I'm glad we're getting out of this place. Well, I think I'll turn in now."

"I'm not sleepy," said Rainsford. "I'm going to smoke my pipe."

"Good night, then, Rainsford. See you at breakfast."

Rainsford leaned back in a deck chair. He puffed lazily on his pipe. "It's so dark," he thought, "that I could sleep without closing my eyes. The night would be my eyelids."

A sudden sound startled him. It came from off to the right. Again he heard the sound, and again. Somewhere, off in the blackness, someone had fired a gun three times.

Rainsford jumped up and moved quickly to the rail. He strained his eyes but could see nothing. He leaped upon the rail and balanced himself there.

His pipe hit a rope and was knocked from his mouth. He reached out for it. A short cry came from his lips as he realized he had reached too far and had lost his balance. The cry was cut off short as the blood-warm waters of the Caribbean Sea closed over his head.

Rainsford struggled up to the surface and tried to cry out. But the waves from the boat slapped him in the face, and the salt water in his mouth made him gag. Desperately, he began to swim after the boat. But he stopped before he had swum fifty feet.

He knew he must remain calm. It was not the first time he had been in a tight place. The lights of the boat became faint. Then they were blotted out by the night.

Rainsford remembered the shots. They had come from the right, and he began to swim in that direction. He fought the sea for what seemed an endless time. He began to count his strokes. He could do possibly a hundred more and then—.

Rainsford heard a sound. It came out of the darkness. It was a high screaming sound—the sound of an animal, terrified and in pain.

He did not recognize the animal that made that sound. He did not try to. With fresh strength, he swam toward the sound. He heard it again. Then it was cut short by a sharp, crisp noise.

"Pistol shot," thought Rainsford, swimming on.

Ten minutes later, he heard the sea breaking on a rocky shore. He was almost on the rocks before he saw them. On a night less calm, he would have been smashed against them. He dragged himself up over the rocks. Finally, he reached a flat place at the top. He knew that he was safe from his enemy, the sea. Thick jungle came down to the cliffs. He threw himself down at the jungle edge and fell into the deepest sleep of his life.

When he opened his eyes, he knew from the position of the sun that it was late in the afternoon. Sleep had given him new strength. He was very hungry.

Rainsford looked around, almost cheerfully.

"Where there are pistol shots, there are men. Where there are men, there is food," he thought. "But what kind of men live in a place like this?"

He saw no sign of a trail through the jungle. It was easier to go along the shore. He began to walk. Not far from where he had landed, he stopped.

Some wounded thing—a large animal, it seemed—had been there. The jungle weeds were crushed down, and one patch of weeds was stained red. Something small and shining caught Rainsford's eye. He picked it up. It was a bullet shell.

"A twenty-two," he said to himself. "That's funny. The hunter had his nerve to take on so large an animal with such a small gun. It's clear it must have put up a good fight."

He examined the ground closely and found the print of hunting boots. They pointed along the cliff in the direction he had been going. He hurried quickly along. Night was beginning to settle.

Darkness was blacking out the sea and jungle when Rainsford sighted lights. His eyes made out the shadowy outlines of a castle. It was set on a high hill. On three sides of it, cliffs dived down to the sea.

"I'm seeing things," thought Rainsford. But it was real enough, he found, when he got to the huge wooden door.

He lifted the knocker and let it fall loudly. The door opened and Rainsford saw the largest man he had ever seen. He was broad and powerful and had a large beard that hung to his waist. In his hand the man held a revolver. And he was pointing it straight at Rainsford's heart.

"Don't be alarmed," said Rainsford. "I'm no robber. I fell off a boat. My name is Sanger Rainsford of New York."

The man's answer was to raise with his thumb the hammer of his revolver. Then, suddenly, the man's other hand went to his forehead. He clicked his heels together and saluted. Another man was coming down the marble steps. He was dressed in evening clothes. He walked over to Rainsford and shook his hand.

He spoke in a cool, smooth voice with a slight accent.

"It is a great honor to welcome Mr. Sanger Rainsford, the famous hunter, to my home."

Rainsford shook the man's hand.

"I've read your book about hunting leopards in Tibet, you see," explained the man. "I am General Zaroff."

Rainsford's first thought was that the man was very handsome. His sec-

ond was that there was something strange about the general's face. He was a tall man past middle age. His hair was bright white, but his thick eyebrows and pointed mustache were as black as the night from which Rainsford had come. His eyes, too, were black and very bright. He had the face of a man used to giving orders.

5

Turning to the giant, the general made a sign. The giant put away his pistol.

"Ivan is a very strong fellow," said the general, "but he is deaf and dumb."

"Is he Russian?"

"He is," said the general. "So am I. I was about to have my dinner when you came. Please join me."

Rainsford followed the general to a magnificent dining room. On the walls were the mounted heads of many animals—lions, tigers, elephants, bears.

The meal was delicious, but there was one small thing that made Rainsford feel funny. Whenever he looked up from his plate, he found the general studying him closely.

"Perhaps," said General Zaroff, "you were surprised that I recognized your name. You see, I read all the books on hunting. I have but one pleasure in my life, and that is the hunt."

"You have some wonderful heads here," said Rainsford. "That Cape buffalo is the largest I ever saw."

"Yes, he was a monster."

"I've always thought," said Rainsford, "that the Cape buffalo is the most dangerous of all big game."

For a moment the general did not answer. He was smiling a strange smile. Then he said slowly, "No. You are wrong, sir. The Cape buffalo is not the most dangerous game." He sipped his wine. "Here, on this island, I hunt more dangerous game."

Rainsford was surprised. "Is there big game on this island?"

The general nodded. "The biggest. I have to bring it here, of course."

"And what have you brought, general?" Rainsford asked. "Tigers?"

The general smiled. "No," he said, "hunting tigers stopped interesting me years ago. There's no thrill left in tigers, no real danger. I live for danger, Mr. Rainsford."

The general lit a long cigarette. "We will have some wonderful hunting, you and I," he said. "I shall be very glad to have your company."

"But what game—" began Rainsford.

"I will tell you," said the general. "You will be amused, I know. I think I have done a rare thing. I have invented a new animal to hunt."

"A new animal? You're joking."

"Not at all," said the general. "I never joke about hunting. I needed a new animal. I found one. So I bought this island. I built this house, and here I do my hunting."

"But the animal, General Zaroff?"

"Oh," said the general, "it gives me the most exciting hunting in the world. Every day I hunt, and I never grow bored."

Rainsford stared at the general.

→ "Yes, I wanted the ideal animal to hunt. So I asked myself 'what qualities must it have?' And the answer was simple. 'It must have courage and be clever. But above all, it must be able to reason.'"

"But no animal can reason," said Rainsford.

"My dear fellow," said the general, "there is one that can."

"But you can't mean—" gasped Rainsford.

"And why not?"

"I can't believe you are serious, General Zaroff. This is some terrible joke."

"Why should I not be serious? I am speaking of hunting."

"Hunting!" cried Rainsford. "What you speak of is murder!"

The general laughed. "You'll see. You'll change your tune when you go hunting with me. You have a new thrill in store for you, Mr. Rainsford."

"I'm a hunter—not a murderer!" answered Rainsford.

"Listen," said the general, "life is for the strong, to be lived by the strong. The weak were put here to give the strong pleasure. I am strong. I wish to hunt. Why shouldn't I? I hunt the trash of the earth—sailors who are lost from their ships."

"But they are *men*," said Rainsford, angrily.

"Exactly," said the general. "That is why I use them. They can reason. So they are dangerous."

"But where do you get them?"

"This island is called Ship Trap," he said. "Sometimes the high seas send them to me. Sometimes I help myself. Come to the window with me."

Rainsford went to the window and looked out toward the sea.

"Watch! Out there!" exclaimed the general, pointing into the night.

Rainsford saw only blackness. Then the general pressed a button. Far out at sea, Rainsford saw a flash of lights.

The general laughed. "The lights show the way to a channel where there is none. There are only rocks that smash the ships. Oh, yes, I use electricity. We are civilized here."

"Civilized? And you shoot down men?"

There was anger in the general's black eyes. "I treat these visitors well. They get plenty of good food and exercise. They get into very good shape. You'll see for yourself tomorrow."

"What do you mean?"

"We'll visit my training school," smiled the general. "It's in the cellar. I have about a dozen pupils down there now. They're from a ship that had the bad luck to go against the rocks.

"It's a game, you see. I suggest to one of them that we go hunting. I give him a supply of food and a hunting knife. I give him a three-hour head start. Then I follow with a pistol. If he can escape from me for three whole days, he wins the game. If I find him"—the general smiled—"he loses."

"Suppose he refuses to be hunted?"

"Oh," said the general, "I give him his choice. If he does not wish to hunt, I turn him over to Ivan. Mr. Rainsford, they always choose the hunt."

"And if they win?"

"So far I have not lost," he said.

"One almost did win. I had to use the dogs."

"The dogs?"

"This way, please. I'll show you."

The general led Rainsford to a window. Below, in the courtward, Rainsford saw a dozen or so huge shapes moving about. Their eyes glittered greenly.

"A rather good lot, I think," said the general. "They are let out at seven every night. If anyone should try to get into my house—or out of it—something very sad would happen to him.

"And now," said the general, "I want to show you my new collection of heads. Will you come with me to the library?"

"I hope," said Rainsford, "that you will excuse me tonight, General Zaroff. I am really not feeling very well."

"That's only natural after your long swim. You need a good night's sleep. Tomorrow you'll feel like a new man. Then we'll hunt, eh?"

Rainsford was hurrying from the room.

"Sorry you can't go with me tonight," called the general. "I expect rather good sport. Well, good night, Mr. Rainsford. I hope you have a good night's rest."

The bed was good. The pajamas were made of the softest silk. But Rainsford could not sleep. He tried to open the door. It would not open. He went to the window and looked out. Below, he saw the dogs, weaving in and out in the courtyard. They heard him and looked up with their green eyes. He finally fell asleep just as morning came. Then he was awakened by a gunshot off in the jungle.

General Zaroff did not appear until lunch. He asked about Rainsford's health. "As for me," said the general, "I do not feel so well. I am afraid I am growing bored."

"What do you mean?" asked Rainsford.

"The hunting was not good last night. The fellow lost his head. He gave me no problem at all."

"General," said Rainsford, "I wish to leave this island at once."

The general seemed hurt. "But my dear fellow, you've only just come. You've had no hunting."

"I wish to go today," said Rainsford.

He saw the black eyes of the general on him.

"Tonight," said the general, "we will hunt—you and I."

Rainsford shook his head. "No, general," he said. "I will not hunt."

The general shrugged his shoulders. "As you wish, my friend," he said. "The choice rests with you. But you will find my idea of sport better than Ivan's."

He nodded to the corner where the giant stood, his thick arms crossed on his chest.

"You don't mean-" cried Rainsford.

"My dear fellow," said the general, "I always mean what I say about hunting. This is really marvelous! An opponent worthy of me—at last. You'll find the game worth playing. Your brain against mine. Your ability and strength against mine. Outdoor chess!"

"And if I win—" began Rainsford.

"I'll admit defeat if I do not find you by midnight of the third day," said General Zaroff. "My boat will take you to the mainland."

The general knew what Rainsford was thinking.

"Oh, you can trust me," he said. "I give you my word as a gentleman and a sportsman. Of course you, in turn, must agree to say nothing of your visit here."

"I'll agree to nothing of the kind," said Rainsford.

"Oh," said the general, "in that case—. But why discuss that now? Ivan will give you hunting clothes, food, and a knife. I suggest you wear moccasins. They leave a poorer trail. I suggest, too, that you stay away from the big swamp in the southeast corner of the island. There's quicksand there.

"Well, I must beg you to excuse me now. I always take a nap after lunch. You'll hardly have time for a nap, I'm afraid. You'll want to start right away, no doubt. I shall not follow till dark. Hunting at night is so much more exciting than by day. Good-bye, Mr. Rainsford. Good-bye."

Focus on the Story

A short story usually contains just one main idea. There are only one or two main characters in a short story. Short stories are considered fiction. This means that they tell about imaginary characters and events.

The **plot** of a story is the outline of events. It is the action in the order in which it happened.

▶ **1.** What happened *first* in the plot of ''The Most Dangerous Game''?
a. Rainsford met General Zaroff.
b. Rainsford fell into the sea.
c. Ivan pointed a revolver at Rainsford.

The **main character** of a story is the person who the story is mostly about. A story can have more than one main character.

▶ **2.** Who are the main characters in the story?
a. Rainsford and Whitney
b. Ivan and General Zaroff
c. Rainsford and General Zaroff

The way an author shows what a character is like is called **characterization.** The way a person looks, talks, acts, or thinks is part of his or her characterization.

▶ **3.** Which sentence best describes General Zaroff?
a. He was twenty-five years of age.
b. He was a tall, handsome man with white hair and a mustache.
c. He was a short man.

Focus on the Language

A **simile** compares two unlike things using the words *like* or *as*.

Examples:
• Their voices boomed like thunder.
• She was graceful as a deer.

▶ **1.** Which sentence from ''The Most Dangerous Game'' contains a simile?
a. He fought the sea for an endless time.
b. The night was like a wet, dark blanket.
c. He puffed lazily on his pipe.

A **metaphor** compares two unlike things without using the words *like* or *as*.

Examples:
• All the world's a stage.
• His fingers were icicles.

▶ **2.** Following are three descriptive statements. Which one contains a metaphor?
a. He had thick eyebrows and a pointed mustache.
b. He spoke in a cool, smooth voice.
c. The night would be my eyelids.

10

The Most Dangerous Game

(Part 2)

Richard Connell

Rainsford took up his flight again.
He ran on for hours. Dusk came, then
darkness. But still, he moved on.

Rainsford had fought his way through the jungle for two hours. "I must keep my nerve. I must keep my nerve," he said through tight teeth.

His whole idea at first was to get as far away from General Zaroff as possible. Now he got a grip on himself and stopped. He saw that plan would bring him face-to-face with the sea.

"I'll give him an impossible trail to follow," Rainsford thought. He left the path he had been following and went off into the wilderness. He made a series of tricky loops and doubled on his trail again and again.

By night, he was very tired. His hands and face were cut by the branches. He knew it would be crazy to go on in the dark. He needed to rest. A big tree was nearby. Taking care not to leave the slightest mark, he climbed up. He stretched out on one of the limbs. He felt better. Not even General Zaroff could follow him there. It was impossible to follow that trail through the jungle after dark.

The night crept by slowly. Rainsford couldn't sleep.

Toward morning, he heard the cry of a bird. Something was coming through the jungle. It was coming slowly, coming carefully, coming by the same winding way that Rainsford had come.

Rainsford flattened himself down on the limb and watched. The thing that was heading towards him was a man!

It was General Zaroff. He made his way along with his eyes fixed on the ground. He stopped, almost beneath the tree. The general studied the ground.

Rainsford's first thought was to leap down like a panther. But he saw that the general held something shiny—a small pistol.

General Zaroff shook his head several times, as if he were puzzled. Rainsford held his breath. The general's eyes had left the ground. They were moving inch by inch up the tree. Rainsford froze there, ready to jump.

But the sharp eyes of the hunter stopped before they reached Rainsford. The general smiled. Then, very slowly, he turned his back to the tree and walked away.

The air burst from Rainsford's lungs. He began to think hard. The general could follow a difficult trail through the woods at night. But why had the general smiled? Why had he turned away?

The truth came to him. The general was playing with him! The general was saving him for another day's sport. General Zaroff was the cat and he was the mouse. At that moment, Rainsford knew the full meaning of terror.

"I will not lose my nerve," he said to himself.

He slid down from the tree and headed off into the woods. Three hundred yards from his hiding place, he stopped. A huge dead tree was leaning against a smaller, living one. Rainsford took out his knife and began to work with all his might.

The job was finished at last! He threw himself down behind a log a hundred feet away. He did not have to wait long.

Down the trail, like a bloodhound, came General Zaroff. He was moving quickly. The general was upon the trap Rainsford had made. His foot touched the branch that was the trigger.

The general sensed his danger and leaped back. But he was not quick enough. The dead tree crashed down and hit him on the shoulder.

He staggered, but he did not fall. Nor did he drop his gun. He stood there, rubbing his injured shoulder. Rainsford heard the general's laugh ring through the jungle.

"Rainsford," called the general, "if you are within the sound of my voice, as I suppose you are, let me congratulate you. Not many men know how to make a Malay man-catcher. Luckily, for me, I too have hunted in Malacca. You are proving interesting, Mr. Rainsford. I am going now to have my wound taken care of. It is only a slight one. But I shall be back. I shall be back!"

Rainsford took up his flight again. He ran on for hours. Dusk came, then darkness. But still, he moved on.

The ground grew softer under his feet. Then, as he stepped forward, his foot sank into the ooze. With a violent effort, he tore his foot loose. He knew now where he was—in the swamp with its quicksand.

The softness of the earth gave Rainsford an idea. He stepped back from the quicksand a dozen feet or so. He began to dig a deep pit. When it was above his shoulders, he climbed out. He took some long, thin branches and sharpened them to a point. He planted these stakes in the bottom of the pit with the points sticking up. He covered the pit with weeds and branches. Then he hid and waited.

Rainsford heard the sound of feet on the soft earth. It seemed to Rainsford that the general was coming very quickly. Rainsford could not see the general or the pit. But he heard the sound of the breaking branches. Then he heard the sharp scream of pain as the pointed stakes found their mark.

Rainsford felt like crying with joy. He leaped up from his hiding place. Then he jumped back. Three feet from the pit a man was standing, holding a flashlight in his hand.

"You've done well, Rainsford," the voice of the general called. "Your Burmese tiger pit has killed one of my best dogs. I think I'll see what you can do against my whole pack. I'm going home now. Thank you for a most amusing evening."

At daybreak, Rainsford was awakened by a fearful sound. It was the barking of a pack of dogs. Rainsford knew he could do one of two things. He could stay where he was and wait. That was suicide. He could run. That would only put off the end.

For a moment he stood there, thinking. An idea came to him, and he headed away from the swamp. The barking of the dogs grew nearer. Rainsford climbed a tree and looked down. Less than a quarter of a mile away, he saw the figure of General Zaroff. Just ahead of him was the giant, Ivan, holding the pack of dogs by a leash.

They would be on him any minute now. He thought of a trick he had learned in Uganda. He slid down and caught hold of a springy young tree. He tied his hunting knife to it, with the blade pointing down the trail. With a piece of vine, he tied back the tree. Then he ran for his life. The dogs were almost there.

He had to stop to get his breath. The barking of the dogs stopped suddenly. They must have reached the knife! He climbed up a tree and looked back. General Zaroff was still on his feet. But Ivan was not. The knife, thrown by the force of the springing tree, had not completely failed.

Rainsford had hardly reached the ground, when the dogs began to bark again.

"Nerve. Keep your nerve," Rainsford told himself, as he dashed along.

He could see something blue between the trees up ahead. Rainsford forced himself toward it. He

reached it. It was the shore of the sea. On the other side, he could see the gray stone of the castle. Twenty feet below him, the sea rumbled and hissed. Rainsford looked below him and hesitated. He heard the barking of the dogs. Then he jumped far out into the sea.

When General Zaroff and his dogs reached the place by the sea, the general stopped. For several minutes he stood looking at the water. He shrugged his shoulders. Then he sat down. He took a drink of brandy from a silver flask. He lit a cigarette and hummed a tune.

General Zaroff had a very fine dinner that evening. He also had a bottle of excellent wine. But two small things kept him from being perfectly happy. One was that it would be hard to replace Ivan. The other was that Rainsford had again escaped him.

At ten o'clock, he went up to his bedroom. He was very tired as he locked himself in. He went to the window and looked down at the courtyard. He could see the dogs. "Better luck next time," he called to them. Then he switched on the light.

A man who had been hiding in the room was standing there.

"Rainsford!" screamed the general. "How did you get here?"

"I swam," said Rainsford. "It was quicker than walking through the jungle."

The general sucked in his breath and smiled. "I congratulate you," he said. "You have won the game."

Rainsford did not smile. "I am still a hunted animal," he said in a low voice. "*Get ready*, General Zaroff."

The general made a deep bow. "I see," he said. "Splendid! One of us will be a meal for the dogs. The other will sleep in this excellent bed. *On guard*, Rainsford."

He had never slept in a better bed, Rainsford thought later.

About the Author

Richard Connell (1893-1949) ⸻

Richard Connell began his writing career as a reporter on his father's newspaper in Poughkeepsie, New York. Following his graduation from Harvard University, Connell worked as a reporter on the *New York American* and as a copywriter for an advertising agency. When World War I broke out, he enlisted and served in France. After Connell returned home, he decided to make writing his career.

Connell has written many short stories and novels. He is also the author of a number of screen plays for motion pictures, including *Meet John Doe*. "The Most Dangerous Game," Connell's most famous short story, won the O. Henry Memorial Award in 1924.

Focus on the Story

The plot of a story is made up of episodes. An **episode** is an incident or an event in the story.

▶ **1.** Which of the following episodes happened *last* in the story?
a. Rainsford made a Malay man-catcher.
b. Rainsford challenged General Zaroff.
c. Rainsford leaped into the sea to escape.

Many stories contain a conflict between characters. A **conflict** is a fight or a difference of opinion.

▶ **2.** The conflict in "The Most Dangerous Game" is between _____ .
a. Ivan and General Zaroff
b. Rainsford and General Zaroff
c. Whitney and Ivan

A **motive** is the reason behind a character's action.

▶ **3.** Why didn't the general kill Rainsford when he first tracked him to the tree?
a. The general was saving Rainsford for another day's sport.
b. The general was afraid of Rainsford.
c. The general wasn't sure that Rainsford was there.

An author sometimes gives clues about what will happen later in the story. This is called **foreshadowing.**

▶ **4.** Which of the following episodes from Part 1 foreshadowed that Rainsford would be hunted in Part 2 of the story?
a. when the general said, "I have invented a new animal to hunt."
b. when Whitney said, "The place has a bad reputation."
c. when Rainsford said, "I fell off a boat."

Focus on the Language

Some words sound like the things they describe. When a word copies a sound, this is known as **onomatopoeia.**

Examples:
- The arrow *whizzed* by.
- The wind *howled* all night.

Simile

A noun is the name of a person, place, thing, or idea.

Examples:
- Ivan
- Ship Trap Island
- gun
- freedom

▶ **1.** In the following sentence, which words are examples of onomatopoeia?
Twenty feet below him, the sea rumbled and hissed.
a. twenty, below
b. feet, sea
c. rumbled, hissed

▶ **2.** Which sentence contains a simile?
a. The softness of the earth gave Rainsford an idea.
b. Down the trail, like a bloodhound, came General Zaroff.
c. The general sucked in his breath and smiled.

▶ **3.** Which words in the following sentence are nouns?
"I must keep my nerve," he said through tight teeth.
a. said, must
b. keep, said
c. nerve, teeth

Talk It Over

1. The word "game" in the title of this story can have more than one meaning. *Game* is a contest or struggle. *Game* also means an animal to be hunted. Why is "The Most Dangerous Game" an especially good title for this story?
2. At the beginning of the story, Rainsford asked, "Who cares how a jaguar feels?" After his experiences with General Zaroff, how do you think Rainsford would answer this question?
3. At the end of the story, is there any hint that Rainsford is going to become another General Zaroff?

The Stove

Marjorie Pickthall

The stove roared. Always hungry.
The dried wood burned like straw.
The great iron horror must be fed.
And she had nothing to feed it.

"I'll be back with the doctor. Three days at the latest. I've left you enough wood for three days. You've got grub enough for a month."

Garth looked at her, anxiously. His strong mouth twitched. Suddenly, he leaned forward. He brushed her cheek lightly with his beard. He was not usually so gentle. "I hate to leave you, little girl," he said. "But I guess it's Derek's only chance."

"Of course you must go. It's Derek's only chance." Dorette faced him. Her look was steady. She was pale and her eyes looked sleepy. But she had been born and bred in the wilderness. Although she looked weak, she had a spirit of steel. Then she said, "There'll be nothing for me to do. Nothing but wait."

"Only look after yourself. And keep the stove up."

"I'll do it. And you—if you meet Maxime—"

Suddenly, her brother's eyes looked fiery. His gun shone blue as he gripped it. "If I meet Maxime," he said through his teeth, "it's either him or me!"

Without another word, he turned away. He headed down the forest trail on his way to Mandore.

Dorette watched him as he rode away. Soon, he was just a dark shadow against the trees. All sound, all movement seemed to go down the trail with him. Dorette went into the cabin. The silence outside seemed like her enemy. She locked the door behind her.

The cabin was a good place. The walls were made of red cedar. Fur rugs covered the floor. Red curtains hung on the windows. There were two large rooms. In the center of the larger room stood a great iron stove. In winter, that stove kept them alive. The roar of the fire was like a hungry voice, always calling out. Dorette answered it, feeding it more wood. That was her job now. Until Garth got back, she must feed the stove.

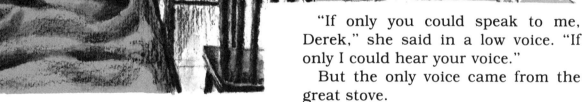

She went to one of the beds and looked down. Derek, her younger brother, lay there. He did not move. He lay as still as he'd been the day Garth carried him in. He was somewhere between life and death. He'd been shot. Now and then, he sipped a bit of soup. But even as he ate, Dorette did not touch him. There was nothing she could do for him. She just had to keep the cabin warm. For the cold of that country kills like a sword.

"If only you could speak to me, Derek," she said in a low voice. "If only I could hear your voice."

But the only voice came from the great stove.

Her mind painted for her the scene she had not witnessed: The hard men of the mines and the lumber camps. Those men following the trail from Fort Dismay to Anisette. The end of the trail at a little lonely shack blinded in snow. Derek pleading that Maxime might have "one more chance, boys." The words at the door. The shot coming from nowhere. Men storming into the shack over Derek's fallen body, and finding it empty. Maxime Dufour escaped again!

She saw it all. Heard again Garth's voice: "But he's not goin' to get away again. He'll have to get food and shelter somewhere. And if it's a thousand miles away, we'll follow and shoot him down like the wolf he is!"

She glanced around, pale and shaken. She thought that she still heard Garth's deep voice of rage. But it was only the roaring stove humming its angry song.

She busied herself with the work she could find. Twice, she fed the stove. The fierce heat licked out at her each time. The fire was like a savage beast striking through the bars of his cage. Each time she shut the door, she had the sense of locking up a living thing.

Her work was soon done. Everything in the cabin was cleaned and cleaned again. She looked at the clock. Only an hour of the slow time had gone. Garth had only been gone an hour! She turned the clock with its face to the wall and took out a shirt she was making for Garth.

Her ears caught the faintest noises. She heard the tiny sound of the thread, passing through the flannel. She heard the soft thud of snow slipping from the trees in the forest. And she always heard Derek's shallow breathing. Her own heart stumbled in tune with it.

So the morning passed. In the afternoon, she found a snow-shoe that needed re-stringing. She twisted the gut and wove the net. In this way, she kept herself busy.

It was dark sooner than she could have hoped. She needed no lamp. The stove filled the cabin with its glow. In the dark, it became a beautiful and living thing. It was a shape of dull red, with a glowing rose heart. She looked at the little windows. They were covered with frost. It would be a cold night. Her thoughts went to Garth. Then, with dread, she thought of Maxime Dufour. She dragged her cot from the inner room. She set it in front of the stove and lay down. The warmth was like a hand pressing on her eyelids.

Even in her sleep, she was watchful of Derek. She was awake five times in the long night to feed the stove. Each time, she looked at Derek. She thought, with a pang, that he was sunken deeper among the pillows. His eyes were not quite closed. His eyeballs reflected the red glow. She would have liked to close them, but her hand shrank from so death-like an action.

The last time she woke, the sun had risen. The frost on the windows was lit by the stove. Dorette went into the inner room and braided her hair.

That day passed as the first had done. Her brother was weaker. She pleaded with him to eat. "Just a mouthful of soup, Derry. Wake up, Derry dear. Take it for my sake, Derry!" But her voice could not reach him now. She looked around for something she might do for him.

There were few logs left. She must bring in a fresh supply from the pile behind the cabin. She ate a quick breakfast. Then, wrapped against the cold, she opened the door.

She stepped into a world of white, blue, and black. It seemed to be built from gems. Where the blue sky touched the black trees, there seemed to run a setting of gold. Where the black trees trailed branches to the snow was a stain of sapphire shadow. She shut the door behind her. She ran to the snow-buried wood-pile behind the cabin. She returned with an armful of small logs and piled the wood on the floor. All the morning, she worked. Her spirits rose. She began to believe that Derek would not die, that Garth would return. The noise of the logs falling to the floor pleased her. It was a change from the one voice that filled the cabin day and night—the voice of the stove.

The second night, she was restless. She dared not sleep at first. She feared she would sleep too well. Wind came up with the stars. The great stove sang a higher note. She could scarcely keep up with its hunger. The pine and birch logs fell to ash in a moment. If she slept, she dreamed that the stove was out. She imagined the cold creeping into the cabin. Long feathers of frost twisted under the door like snakes. One touched her on the throat. She woke, choking.

Dawn found the sky filled with clouds. The cabin was warm. The hurt man was still alive.

Again with the day, her heart lightened. In four or five hours, Garth and the doctor might be there. She wound the clock. She turned it to the room. She no longer dreaded the passage of the hours.

Yet five hours went, and Garth had not come.

She went to the door and stared down the trail. It ran straight for no more than a half-mile. Farther than that, she could not see. Yet it was less her eyes than her soul that strained to see beyond the forest.

"Garth! Garth! Garth!"

Who had cried that among the trees? For a moment, she wondered. Then she knew it had come from her own troubled heart.

She must see beyond the first bend of the trail. She must see if the blue ribbon between the trees was still empty of her hope.

She built up the fire again. Then she put on coat and hood and snow-shoes.

She took one glance at Derek and left the cabin. She sped down the trail. She was panting when she reached the first curve. She was almost afraid to look. She saw the long track before her—empty. There was something deliberate in that emptiness. It was as if the forest withheld from her a secret. She dared go no farther. She turned back and fled home.

The clock ticked off another hour—two, three, four. Garth had not come.

Darkness, and he had not come.

Loneliness was shaking her strong, young nerves. The worst of all was the silence. The voice of the stove became a burden. The voice of its hunger was the voice of silence, of emptiness. She flung the wood in angrily. "If there was only someone to speak to!" she said, a little wildly. "Just someone to give me a word!"

There was no one. She feared to sleep. The stove that kept them alive might escape her. Garth did not come.

There was no wood left in the house. She wrapped herself and went to the wood-pile.

It was heaped against the back of the cabin. The wood was covered with snow. She pulled at a log and the wood fell down. The hard work was a relief to her. She piled such a load that she swayed under it. "But it's something to do for Derek," she said. "It's all I can do."

She took in enough for the day. But there was the night.

"Garth will be back by then," she said, staring at the stove. "Garth must be back by then." The stove sent a screaming rush of flame up the pipe. It seemed to mock her. She felt a hatred for it. But she went out again to gather enough wood for the night too.

She knelt beside the wood-pile. She reached for the logs. But she felt nothing but snow.

She thrust in her arm to the shoulder. Her heart beat in throbs. She brought a long pole and prodded the pile. Then she swung the pole and levelled it. She found nothing but snow.

"How did it happen?" She heard herself asking this over and over. Easily enough. She or Garth or Derek had been drawing supplies from the other side of the pile. The snow had slipped from the roof and filled the spaces. The pile of hardwood logs was no more than a heap of snow.

Dorette turned slowly. She went into the cabin.

She stood by Derek's bunk. She stared at the wood on the floor. It was enough for the day. But what of the night?

Would Garth return before the night?

She looked about the cabin. There were things there, things that would burn. Her sleepy brown eyes widened. There was war in them. She leaned and kissed Derek's cheek. He did not stir from that deep sleep of his.

"Sleep on, Derry," she whispered, hardly knowing what she said. "Sleep well, Derry. I'll take care of you. I'll fight for you!"

She took Garth's heavy ax and began on the chairs.

They were heavy and clumsy things. Garth had made them himself and was proud of them. They would feed the stove well. But they were hard for her to chop. Dorette's hands had been burned from the door of the stove. As she worked, her eyes searched the cabin. This box would do, that shelf, the table. Her heart beat to every sound. The wind rose higher. The bitter day was full of sounds. A dozen times she ran to the door, crying "Garth!" A dozen times she saw nothing. Only the forest and the snow greeted her.

By early evening, she had chopped up everything in the cabin. Each stroke sent pain to her shoulder from her burned hands. But she did not feel it. And still the stove roared. Always hungry. The dried wood burned like straw. The great iron horror must be fed. And she had nothing to feed it.

She took the ax and went out.

The gray forest lay in front of her. There must be a hundred fallen boughs near the cabin. She found one and dragged it from the snow into the house. She pulled it. She twisted it apart. Her hands tore. There was blood on the twigs that she fed to the stove.

She went out again. She was growing more desperate. Her strength failed. There was a great branch trailing from a spruce. She tore at it, but it would not yield. It was frozen. She swung her weight upon it, crying. She struck with all the force left in her. But the ax-blade turned in her tired hands. She felt as though her will alone should cut the bough. She did not know she was beaten until she slipped weakly and fell in the snow and lay there. She sobbed helplessly and softly as a child.

The bitter snow stung her face. If she stayed there, the stove would be out. She lifted herself to her knees. In the growing dark, she saw a man. He stood with a rifle on his arm, looking down at her.

"Garth! Oh, Garth!"

But even as she cried out, she knew it was not Garth.

It was a man, his face hidden under a fur cap. He seemed strangely still—like a wild cat about to attack. But surely, he would help. Wouldn't he?

"The stove! Oh, the stove!"

She thought, as her hands went out to him, that he would understand all that was in her heart. She repeated, "Oh, the stove, the stove!"

"What stove?"

"The stove. The stove in our cabin. There's no more wood for it!"

She waited. Surely he understood. But he remained as he was. He did not move.

She looked up at him. She had forgotten to rise from her knees. She kneeled at his feet in the snow. Her breath came in gasps. "There," she repeated helplessly, "there—in the cabin—the stove! It's going out!"

Still he waited.

"There's a sick man there—my brother! Oh, help me, if you're a man!"

"Oh, b'gosh, yes, I'm a man!" She fancied that he was laughing at her. "But why should I help you?"

She had no more words. Silently she held out her bleeding hands to him.

After a long minute, he stirred slowly. Without a word, he laid his gun on two branches that grew above her reach, but within his own. He lifted the ax from the snow. She watched him. Four sharp cuts and the branch fell. He set his foot on it. He chopped it quickly into four or five pieces. As each piece rolled free, Dorette grabbed it. She was like a starving woman snatching bread.

"That enough?"

She stared at him. "No, no!" she stammered. "It's not enough for the night. Cut me some more!"

She turned away and ran towards the cabin. Halfway there, he overtook her. Without a word, he lifted the logs from her arms into his own. She was too spent to thank him. Dumbly she moved at his side. Help was here. The stove would be fed. She might yet save Derek.

In the cabin, there was no light at all. Dorette swung open the door of the stove. Nothing was there but a handful of red-gray ash.

With trembling hands, she gathered a few splinters and she thrust them in. She crouched before the hungry iron thing. The man, who had followed her, pushed her aside. He shaved a stick into fine ribbons of wood. She watched him coax them into flame. He tickled the appetite of the stove with little twigs. Soon the fire laid hold on the larger logs. It fed upon them, hissing. He shut the door then, and turned to her. She had lit a lamp. In the light she stood looking at him. Her eyes were stars of thanks. She said at once, "My brother's still living."

She gestured towards the bunk. His eyes did not follow her motion. He said abruptly, "You stay here with him. I'm goin' to get you some more wood."

Her eyes flashed suddenly with tears. She said, brokenly, "You're *good*. Oh, you're a good man! While you're cuttin' the wood, I'll—thank God you came!"

He went out into the night without answering her.

He returned in half an hour, loaded mightily. She smiled at him. She had been weeping.

He did not speak to her. He moved as light-footed as a cat. He busied himself about the humming stove. Then he went out again.

When he came back the second time, she was asleep.

Her pale face was rose-colored in the glow of the stove. Her hurt hands were curled within one another. They looked like the hands of a child. Moving in his noiseless way, the man went again. He looked down at her.

His face caught the light of the stove. Dark, keen, and predatory. It was not the face of a man; rather it was the look of hate itself. His movements showed no gentleness. But he seemed gentle when he lifted one of Dorette's dark braids which had fallen to the soiled floor. He placed it on the cot beside her.

Her hair was warm. His hand lingered over it. He leaned above her. Her breath was warm. As if called from her dreams, she awoke. She looked at him with the clear eyes of a child. "I—did thank God—you came," she whispered. Sleep held her again, almost before she had finished speaking.

The young man drew back. He quietly lifted the ax. Once more, he went out.

Silent and untiring, he toiled for her all night. And all night, she slept.

She had slipped into sleep as a child does, worn out and afraid. She woke a woman, and flushed to her hair, as she realized that the stranger had worked while she had slept.

The man was standing in the open doorway. There was a frosty freshness in the air. The world outside was a dazzle of sun. A crow called in the forest. It was the first sun of spring, the year's change. In Dorette's heart, there was a change also. It was the birth of something new and unknown. It almost brought tears to her eyes.

For the first time in her hard life, she had rested on another's strength. She had found it sweet. That simple heart was in her look as she went to the stranger. She said, softly, "I did not mean to sleep. Why did you let me?"

He said, almost roughly. "You were all tired out."

The tears brimmed over. She did not know if pain or happiness moved her. She went on, "I said—I knew—you were a good man."

"Well," he answered, "for one night."

His furred hood hid his face. She said, "Let me see you. Let me see your face."

"Why?"

She was confused. She did not know why. "Because of what you have done—of what we owe you."

"We?"

"My brothers and I. Derek's still alive. I almost think he's sleeping

25

better—more natural. Garth will come home soon. He'll thank you as I'd like to."

She looked up into his face. He had turned from her again. He was gazing down the trail. After a moment, he said, "There's coffee on the back of the stove. And some cornbread. You'd better eat it. I've had some."

She went meekly. She was ashamed that she had slept while the man who had saved her served himself. She would have liked to serve him. Something strange and stormy was shaking her. She had no name for it. The food choked her. But she ate it obediently.

She had hardly finished when he called her. She ran and joined him at the door. Something in his voice thrilled her. She saw in him again that strange cat-like stillness.

He said: "You're lookin' for your brother to come back?"

"Yes, yes. Any time."

"With another man?"

"With the doctor. Why?"

He raised his arm and pointed. In the blinding sun, she saw two small, dark figures, rounding the curve of the trail.

Her heart rose. She was flooded with thankfulness. She said, quietly, after a minute, "Yes, yes, it's him and the doctor. Now—now, you'll let him thank you, as you—won't let me."

Her words ended almost in a question. For she saw that, while she had been eating, he had taken his rifle on his arm and had put on his snow-shoes. Suddenly, she began to tremble a little. She sensed something in his silence. His stillness was somehow threatening.

He swung upon her suddenly. One would have said savagely, except that he was laughing. Those two black figures down the trail were getting nearer. He put a hard, slim hand on Dorette's shoulder. He turned her, so that she faced him. He said softly, in his almost noiseless laughter, "I'll show you how you can thank me."

She looked up at him. Her face was colorless. Her lips parted. In the shadow of the hood, his eyes gleamed at her. His face bent nearer. The world fell away from her. There was nothing left in life for a minute but that face, that voice.

She just breathed, "Who are you?"

"You'll know in a minute!" He looked swiftly from her to the two men down the trail. They were coming on fast. He seemed to be measuring his distance from them.

When they were so near that their faces were almost clear, he caught the girl to him. She was weak in his hold. All her life seemed to be in her dazed eyes. She would have fallen. But he held her with an arm like a steel bar. And twice and three times, he kissed her.

"That's how you can thank me!" He released her, laughing still. She staggered. Her hands touched her red mouth. With the movement of release, he pushed her into the cabin. A bullet sent a spray of dusty snow over him.

She saw, in one instant, Garth on his knee down the trail. His rifle was raised for another shot. The laughing shadow was slipping from her hands, from her life. He moved into the forest from which he had come.

Another shot missed the mark. Garth leapt to his feet. He ran towards her. The doctor followed. But she had no eyes for them. For a moment, she had no heart.

Her eyes and heart were on that other figure at the edge of the trees.

With a terrible laughing, he called to her, *"Tell him you kissed Maxime Dufour!"*

When Garth reached her side, she was on her knees. She was laughing and sobbing. With her small hands, she tried to erase his trail in the snow.

About the Author

Marjorie L.C. Pickthall (1883-1922) ——

Majorie Pickthall was one of Canada's most popular writers. Born in England, she moved to Toronto, Canada, where she spent her childhood. After a stay in England, Pickthall returned to Canada and later made her home in Victoria, British Columbia.

Pickthall loved the mountains and wilderness and found that she did her best work alone, surrounded by nature. Because of this, she built a shack under a tall pine tree. There she did her writing.

Marjorie Pickthall has written poetry as well as short stories. It is for her stories, however, that she is best known. Many of these appeared originally in magazines such as the *Atlantic Monthly, Harper's,* and *Scribners.* In "The Stove," the reader can almost feel the cold of the Canadian Northwest which the author so loved.

Focus on the Story

Main Character

▶ **1.** The main character in "The Stove" is _____.

a. Dorette
b. Garth
c. Maxime Dufour

The **setting** of a story is *where* and *when* the action takes place.

▶ **2.** The setting of "The Stove" is a _____.
a. house in the city
b. cabin in the wilderness
c. lumber camp in the West

Characterization

▶ **3.** Which description best characterizes Dorette?
a. She was brave and determined.
b. She was lazy and unconcerned.
c. She was thoughtless and selfish.

Dialogue is the speech between characters. Dialogue can help characterize the people in the story.

▶ **4.** Maxime said to Dorette, "You stay here with him. I'm goin' to get you some more wood." This dialogue shows that Maxime _____.
a. didn't care about Dorette's problem
b. was able to put Dorette's safety above his own
c. was hoping that Garth would soon return

An **inner conflict** is the conflict in the mind of the character.

▶ **5.** At the conclusion of the story, Garth found Dorette on her knees in the snow. She was "laughing and sobbing." This suggests that Dorette _____.

a. wanted Garth to shoot Maxime Dufour
b. wanted Maxime to shoot Garth
c. had mixed feelings about Dufour

Focus on the Language

Many stories and poems contain **figurative language.** Figurative language is very descriptive, but it is not meant to be taken literally.

Example:
- With fire in his eyes, he watched the scene.

When a writer gives human traits to non-human things, this is known as **personification.**

Examples:
- The flowers danced in the breeze.
- The forest welcomed us.

Metaphor

Simile

▶ **1.** In the story, "Long fingers of frost twisted under the door." This is another way of saying that _____ .

  a. the room became cold
  b. the door was unlocked
  c. her hands were freezing

▶ **2.** Which sentence shows personification?
  a. By evening, she had chopped up everything in the cabin.
  b. He headed down the forest trail.
  c. It was only the roaring stove humming its angry song.

▶ **3.** Following are three statements about Dorette. Which one is a metaphor?
  a. She was like a starving woman snatching bread.
  b. Her eyes were stars of thanks.
  c. She slept as a child, worn out and afraid.

▶ **4.** The stove is described often in this story. Which description contains a simile?
  a. The fire was like a savage beast striking through the bars of his cage.
  b. The great stove sang a higher note.
  c. The voice of the stove became a burden.

Write About It

Unlike the reader, Garth does not know what has happened to Dorette while he was gone. Now that he has returned, Garth will want to learn what her days were like. What do you think Dorette will tell him? In two paragraphs, write *Dorette's* account of what happened while Garth was away. In the first paragraph, describe the events *before* Maxime Dufour's arrival. In the second paragraph, explain what happened *after* Maxime Dufour arrived.

Stopping by Woods on a Snowy Evening

Robert Frost

Whose woods these are I think I know.
His house is in the village, though;
He will not see me stopping here
To watch his woods fill up with snow.

My little horse must think it queer
To stop without a farmhouse near
Between the woods and frozen lake
The darkest evening of the year.

He gives his harness bells a shake
To ask if there is some mistake.
The only other sound's the sweep
Of easy wind and downy flake.

The woods are lovely, dark, and deep,
But I have promises to keep,
And miles to go before I sleep,
And miles to go before I sleep.

Focus on the Poem

Poetry is a special use of language. A poem is meant to be heard—like a song. Listen to how the words sound. Think of the pictures the poet creates.

A **stanza** is a group of lines that goes together. "Stopping by Woods on a Snowy Evening" contains four stanzas. Each stanza is four lines long.

▶ **1.** By reading the first stanza, you can tell that the setting is _____.
a. a village
b. the woods
c. a farmhouse

Imagery is the picture the poet creates in the mind of the reader. Unlike figurative language, imagery *is* meant to be taken literally.

Example:
  • The woods are lovely, dark, and deep.

▶ **2.** In the second stanza, the poet creates an image of a _____.
a. horse standing in a snowcovered, wooded area on a dark night
b. farmer plowing the fields in the daytime
c. lake where people have gathered to go fishing

Rhyme is the repetition of similar sounds.

Example:
  • *Know* rhymes with *though* and *snow.*

▶ **3.** In the third stanza, which words rhyme?
a. *shake, mistake,* and *flake*
b. *only, easy,* and *other*
c. *bells, sound,* and *wind*

The way the author uses language is called the **author's style.** The style includes the author's choice of words and the arrangement of words and sentences.

▶ **4.** What is true of the style of this poem?
a. Each stanza contains at least three rhyming lines.
b. The last two lines are the same.
c. both of the above

An **adjective** is a word that describes a noun.

Examples:
  • *quiet* village
  • *darkest* evening

▶ **5.** In stanza four, which adjectives describe the woods?
a. lovely, dark, deep
b. promises, miles, sleep
c. are, have, go

Unit Review

Write your answers on a separate sheet of paper.

1. "The Stove" is classified as _____.
   a. poetry
   b. a true story
   c. fiction

2. The setting of Part 2 of "The Most Dangerous Game" is _____.
   a. an island
   b. a small town
   c. a ship

3. Which of the following happened last in the plot of "The Stove"?
   a. Garth left to find a doctor.
   b. Dorette kissed Maxime Dufour.
   c. Dorette discovered there were no logs in the wood-pile.

4. When an author gives clues about what will happen later in the story, this is called _____.
   a. characterization
   b. inner conflict
   c. foreshadowing

5. "I always mean what I say about hunting." This line of dialogue was spoken by _____.
   a. Maxime Dufour to Dorette
   b. Rainsford to Ivan
   c. General Zaroff to Rainsford

6. Match each word with its definition.
   a. characterization — a strong difference of opinion between characters __
   b. episode — an incident or event in the plot of the story __
   c. conflict — ways of showing how a character looks, talks, acts or thinks __

Reviewing the Language

1. The sentence, "I am a hunted animal," is an example of _____.
   - **a.** a simile
   - **b.** a metaphor
   - **c.** personification

2. Dorette heard "the soft thud of snow." The word *thud* is an example of _____.
   - **a.** a metaphor
   - **b.** onomatopoeia
   - **c.** personification

3. "The laughing shadow was slipping from her hands, from her life" is figurative language meaning that _____.
   - **a.** Maxime was leaving
   - **b.** it was growing dark
   - **c.** Dorette was very happy with her life

4. Match each word with its definition.
   - **a.** adjective — a word that describes a noun __
   - **b.** imagery — the repetition of similar sounds __
   - **c.** rhyme — the picture the writer creates in the mind of the reader __

Talking It Over

1. This unit is called "On the Run." Think about "The Most Dangerous Game " and "The Stove." How were Rainsford, Maxime Dufour, and Dorette all "on the run"? Which character was in the greatest danger?

2. At the beginning of "The Most Dangerous Game," Whitney and Rainsford discussed hunting. What did their conversation have to do with the rest of the story? Who won "the most dangerous game"? How do you know?

3. Why was Dorette in greater danger than she realized? When did you first suspect who the stranger was? Why did Dufour laugh after kissing Dorette? After Dorette discovered Dufour's identity, she still tried to cover up his tracks. Why?

4. Reread the last stanza of Robert Frost's poem. What "promises" does the poet "have to keep"? What does he mean when he says, "I have miles to go before I sleep"?

unit 2
Holding onto a Dream

Hitch your wagon to a star.
—Ralph Waldo Emerson

Antaeus

Borden Deal

I looked at T.J. then, knowing in a small way the hunger within him, knowing the dream that lay behind his plan. He was a new Antaeus, preparing his own bed of strength.

It was during wartime. Lots of people were coming North for jobs in the factories. People moved around a lot more than they do now. Sometimes kids were thrown into new groups and new lives that were completely different from anything they had ever known before. I remember this one kid. T.J. was his name. He came from somewhere down in the South. His family moved into our building during that time. They'd come up North with everything they owned piled into the back seat of an old car. T.J. and his three younger sisters rode all the way on top of the load of junk.

Our building was just like all the others there. Families were crowded into a few rooms. I guess there were twenty-five or thirty kids about my age in that one building. A few of us formed a gang. We ran together all the time after school. I was the one who brought T.J. in and started the whole thing.

The building right next door to us was a factory. They made walking dolls. It was a low building with a flat roof. No one, not even the watchman, paid any attention to the roof. It was higher than any of the other buildings around. So my gang used the roof as a headquarters. We could get up there by crossing over to the fire escape from our own roof. It was a secret place for us. Nobody else could go there without our say-so.

I remember the day I first took T.J. up there to meet the gang. He was a big kid with white hair. There was nothing sissy about him except his voice. He talked in this slow, gentle voice like you never heard before. He talked different from any of us. You noticed it right away. But I liked him anyway, so I told him to come on up.

We climbed up to the roof. The rest of the gang were already there.

"Hi," I said. I pointed to T.J. "He just moved into the building yesterday."

He just stood there. He wasn't scared or anything. He was just looking, like the first time you see somebody you're not sure you're going to like.

"Hi," Blackie said. "Where you from?"

"Marion County," T.J. said.

We laughed. "Marion County?" I said. "Where's that?"

He looked at me for a moment like I was a stranger, too. "It's in Alabama," he said, like I ought to know where it was.

"What's your name?" Charley said.

"T.J.," he answered.

"T.J.," Blackie said. "That's just initials. What's your real name? Nobody in the world has just initials."

"I do," he said. "And they're T.J. That's all the name I got."

His voice was firm. For a moment no one had anything to say. T.J. looked around at the rooftop. "Down yonder where I come from," he said, "we played out in the woods. Don't you-all have no woods around here?"

"Naw," Blackie said. "There's the park a few blocks over. But it's full of kids and cops and old women. You can't do a thing."

T.J. kept looking at the tar under his feet. "You mean you ain't got no fields to raise nothing in?—no watermelons or nothing?"

"Naw," I said. "What do you want to grow something for? The folks can buy everything they need at the store."

He looked at me again with that strange look. "In Marion County," he said, "I had my own land for growing cotton and my own land for growing corn. It was mine to plant and make ever' year."

He sounded like it was something to be proud of. In some way, it made the rest of us angry. Blackie said, "Who'd want to have their own land for cotton and corn? That's just work. What can you do with it?"

T.J. looked at him. "Well, you get part of the bale offen your acre," he said. "And I fed my acre of corn to my calf."

We didn't really know what he was talking about, so were more puzzled than angry. Otherwise, I guess, we'd have chased him off the roof and wouldn't let him be part of our gang. But he was strange and different, and we were all attracted by his sense of rightness and belonging. Or maybe we liked the strange softness of his voice. It was so different from our own harsh tones of speech.

He moved his foot against the black tar. "We could make our own field right here," he said softly. "Come spring we could raise us what we want to—watermelons and vegetables. There's no telling what all."

"You'd have to be a good farmer to make these tar roofs grow any watermelons," I said. We all laughed.

But T.J. looked serious. "We could haul us some dirt up here," he said, "and spread it out even and water it. Before you know it, we'd have us a crop in here." He looked closely at us. "Wouldn't that be fun?"

"They wouldn't let us," Blackie said quickly.

"I thought you said this was you-all's roof," T.J. said to me, "that you-all could do anything you wanted to up here."

"They've never bothered us," I said. I felt the idea beginning to catch fire in me. It was a big idea. It took a while for it to sink in, but the more I thought about it, the better I liked it. "Say," I said to the gang. "He might have something there. Just make us a regular roof garden, with flowers and grass and trees and everything. And all ours, too," I said. "We wouldn't let anybody up here except the ones we wanted to."

"It'd take a while to grow trees," T.J. said quickly. But by then we weren't paying any attention to him. We were all talking about the plan. Everyone was all excited with the idea after I'd put it in a way they could catch hold of it. Only rich people had

roof gardens, we knew. The idea of our own private garden excited us.

"We could bring it up in sacks and boxes," Blackie said. "We'd have to do it while the folks weren't paying any attention to us."

"Where could we get the dirt?" somebody said.

"Out of those empty lots over close to school," Blackie said. "Nobody'd notice if we dug it up."

I slapped T.J. on the shoulder. "Man, you had a wonderful idea," I said. Everybody grinned at him, remembering that he had started it. "Our own private roof garden."

He grinned back. "It'll be our'n," he said. "All our'n." Then he looked thoughtful again. "Maybe I can lay my hands on some cotton seed, too. You think we could raise us some cotton?"

We'd started big projects before at one time or another, like any gang of kids. But they'd always fallen apart.

38

But this one didn't. Somehow or other, T.J. kept it going all through the winter. He kept talking about the watermelons and the cotton we'd raise, come spring. And when even that wouldn't work, he'd switch around to my idea of flowers and grass and trees. But he was always honest enough to add that it'd take a while to get any trees started. He always had it on his mind, and he'd mention it in school. He wanted to get other kids lined up to carry dirt, too. He reckoned a few more weeks ought to see the job through.

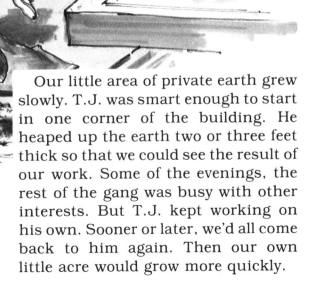

Our little area of private earth grew slowly. T.J. was smart enough to start in one corner of the building. He heaped up the earth two or three feet thick so that we could see the result of our work. Some of the evenings, the rest of the gang was busy with other interests. But T.J. kept working on his own. Sooner or later, we'd all come back to him again. Then our own little acre would grow more quickly.

He was careful about the kind of dirt he'd let us carry up there. More than once he dumped a sandy load off the roof into the areaway below. It wasn't good enough, he said. He found out the kinds of earth in all the empty lots for blocks around. He'd pick it up and feel it and smell it, even if it was frozen. Then he'd say it was good growing soil or it wasn't worth anything, and we'd have to go on somewhere else.

Thinking about it now, I don't see how he kept us at it. It was hard work. We had to lug paper sacks and boxes of dirt all the way up the stairs of our own building, keeping out of the way of the grownups. They probably wouldn't have cared. They didn't pay much attention to us, but we wanted to keep it secret anyway. Then we had to go through the trapdoor to our roof, walk over a plank to the fire escape, and then drop down onto the roof. All that for a small pile of earth that sometimes didn't seem worth the effort. But T.J. kept the vision bright within us. He worked harder than any of us. He seemed driven toward a goal that we couldn't see.

The earth just lay there during the cold months, lifeless. The clods were lumpy and cold under our feet when we walked over it. But one day it rained. Afterward, there was a softness in the air. The earth was live and giving again with moisture and warmth.

That evening, T.J. smelled the air, filling his nostrils with the odor of the earth under his feet. "It's spring," he said. There was a gladness in his voice. It filled us all with the same feeling. "It's mighty late for it, but it's spring. I'd just about decided it wasn't never gonna get here at all."

We were all sniffing at the air, too, trying to smell it the way that T.J. did. I can still remember the sweet odor of the earth under our feet. It was the first time in my life that spring and spring earth had meant anything to me. I looked at T.J. then, knowing in a small way the hunger within him, knowing the dream that lay behind his plan. He was a new Antaeus, preparing his own bed of strength.

"Planting time," he said. "We'll have to find us some seed."

"What do we do?" Blackie said. "How do we do it?"

"First we'll have to break up the clods," T.J. said. "That won't be hard to do. Then we plant the seeds. After a while, they come up. Then you got you a crop." He frowned. "But you ain't got it raised yet. You got to tend it and hoe it and take care of it. All the time, it's growing and growing, even while you're awake and while you're asleep. Then you lay it by when it's growed and let it ripen. And then you got you a crop."

"There's those seed houses over on Sixth," I said. "We could probably swipe some grass seed over there."

T.J. looked at the earth. "You-all seem mighty set on raising some grass," he said. "I ain't never put no

40

effort into that. I spent all my life trying *not* to raise grass."

"But it's pretty," Blackie said. "We could play on it and take sun-baths on it. Like having our own lawn. Lots of people got lawns."

"Well," T.J. said. He looked at us, unsure for the first time. He kept on looking at us for a moment. "I did have it in mind to raise some vegetables. But we'll plant grass."

He was smart. He knew where to give in. And I don't suppose it made any difference to him, really. He just wanted to grow something, even if it was grass.

"Of course," he said, "I do think we ought to plant a row of watermelons. They'd be mighty nice to eat while we was a-laying on that grass."

We all laughed. "All right," I said. "We'll plant us a row of watermelons."

Things went very quickly then. Half the roof was covered with the earth. We swiped pocketfuls of grass seed from the open bins in the seed house. T.J. showed us how to get the earth ready. It looked rich and black now, ready to receive the seed. It seemed that the grass sprang up overnight, pale green in the early spring.

We couldn't keep from looking at it. It was hard to believe that we had made this soft growth. We looked at T.J. with understanding now. We knew the fulfillment of the plan he had carried along within his mind. We had worked without full understanding of the task. But he had known all the time.

We found that we couldn't walk or play on the delicate blades. But we didn't mind. It was enough just to look at it. It was enough to realize that it was the work of our own hands. Each evening, the whole gang was there. We were trying to measure the growth that had taken place that day.

One time, a foot was placed on the plot of ground, one time only. Blackie stepped onto it with sudden bravado. Then he looked at the crushed blades. There was shame in his face. He did not do it again. This was his grass, too. It was not to be treated badly. No one said anything, for it was not necessary.

T.J. had kept a small section for watermelons. He was still trying to find some seed for it. The seed house didn't have any watermelon seeds. We didn't know where we could lay our hands on them.

We had just about decided that we'd have to buy the seeds if we were to get them. It was against our way of doing things, but we were in a hurry to get the watermelons started. One day, T.J. got his hands on a seed catalog. He brought it to our roof garden.

"We can order them now," he said, showing us the book. "Look!"

We all crowded around, looking at the fat watermelons pictured in full color on the pages. Some of them were split open, showing the red meat. The pictures made our mouths water.

"Now we got to scrape up some seed money." T.J. said, looking at us. "I got a quarter. How much you-all got?"

We made up a couple of dollars among us. T.J. nodded his head. "That'll be more than enough. Now we got to decide what kind to get. I think them Kleckley Sweets. What do you-all think?"

He was going into things beyond our reach. We hadn't even known there were different kinds of melons, so we just nodded our heads. We agreed that yes, we thought the Kleckley Sweets too.

"I'll order them tonight," T.J. said. "We ought to have them in a few days."

"What are you boys doing up here?" an adult voice said behind us.

It startled us. No one had ever come up here before in all the time we had been using the roof. We turned around. Three men were standing near the trap door at the other end of the roof. They weren't policemen or night watchmen. They wore business suits. They were looking at us. They walked toward us.

"What are you boys doing up here?" the one in the middle said again.

We stood still. Guilt was heavy among us. We didn't really feel guilty. But the man's voice told us we should be feeling it.

The men stared at the grass growing behind us. "What's this?" the man said. "How did this get up here?"

"Sure is growing good, ain't it?" T.J. said. "We planted it."

The men kept looking at the grass as if they didn't believe it. It was a thick carpet over the earth now. The patch of greenness stood out above the city surroundings.

"Yes, sir," T.J. said proudly. "We toted that earth up here and planted that grass." He showed them the seed catalog. "And we're just fixing to plant us some watermelon."

The man looked at him then, his eyes strange and faraway. "What do you mean, putting this on the roof of my building?" he said. "Do you want to go to jail?"

T.J. looked shaken. The rest of us were silent. We were frightened by the sound of his voice. We had grown up aware of that adult voice. Policemen and night watchmen and teachers all had it. And this man sounded like all the others. But it was a new thing to T.J.

"Well, you wasn't using the roof," T.J. said. He waited a moment and added, "So we just thought to pretty it up a little bit."

"And sag it so I'd have to rebuild it," the man said sharply. He started turning away. To another man beside him he said, "See that all that junk is shoveled off by tomorrow."

"Yes, sir," the man said.

T.J. started forward. "You can't do that," he said. "We toted it up here. It's our earth. We planted it and raised it and toted it up here."

The man stared at him coldly. "But it's my building," he said. "It's to be shoveled off tomorrow."

"It's our earth," T.J. cried. "You ain't got no right!"

The men walked on without listening. They climbed down through the trapdoor. T.J. stood looking after them. His body was tense with anger. They wouldn't even argue with him. They wouldn't let him fight for his earth-rights.

He turned to us. "We won't let 'em do it," he said. "We'll stay up here all day tomorrow. And the day after that. We won't let 'em do it."

We just looked at him. We knew there was no stopping it.

He saw it in our faces. His face changed for a moment. Then he became determined again. "They ain't got no right," he said. "It's our earth. It's our land. Can't nobody touch a man's own land."

We kept looking at him. We listened to the words, but we knew that it was no use. The adult world had come down on us. Even our richest dream was not rich enough to stop them. We knew there was no fighting. There was no winning against it.

We started moving slowly toward the fire escape. We didn't take a last look at the green beauty of earth that T.J. had planted for us. He had planted more than grass. He had planted something important in our minds. We filed slowly over the edge and down the steps to the plank. T.J. came last. All of us could feel the weight of his grief behind us.

"Wait," he said suddenly. His voice was harsh with the effort of calling.

We stopped and turned. We were held by the tone of his voice. We looked up at him standing above us on the fire escape.

"We can't stop them?" he said. He was looking down at us, his face strange in the evening light. "There ain't no way to stop 'em?"

"No," Blackie said. "They own the building."

We stood still for a moment, looking up at T.J. We could see something working in his face. He stared back at us. His face was pale and mean in the poor light.

"They ain't gonna touch my earth," he said. "They ain't gonna lay a hand on it! Come on."

He turned around and started up the fire escape again. He was almost running. We followed more slowly, not knowing what he was thinking. By the time we reached him, he had a board in his hand. He dug it into the soil. Scoop by scoop, he threw it off the roof into the areaway below. He straightened and looked at us.

"They can't touch it," he said. "I won't let 'em lay a dirty hand on it!"

We saw it then. He stooped to his work again. We followed. The gusts of his anger blew among us. Each of us helped scoop up the earth. We threw the soil over the edge of the roof. In anger, we destroyed the growth we had made with such tender care. The

green blades of grass fell to the area-way below.

It took less time than you would think. It is easier to destroy than to build. When it was finally over, a stillness stood among the group and over the building. We looked down at the black tar. We felt the harsh texture of it under the soles of our shoes. The anger had gone out of us. Only a sore aching was left in our minds.

T.J. stood for a moment, his breathing slowed. He stooped slowly. Finally he picked up a lonely blade of grass. He put it between his teeth, tasting it, sucking the greenness out of it into his mouth. Then he started walking toward the fire escape. He moved before any of us were ready to move. He disappeared over the edge.

We followed him. But he was already halfway to the ground. He stood on the concrete below us and looked at the small pile of earth. Then he walked across the place where we could see him. He disappeared toward the street without looking back. He didn't see us watching him.

They did not find him for two weeks.

Then the Nashville police caught him just outside the Nashville train yards. He was walking along the track. He was heading south, still heading home.

As for us, we had no remembered home to call us. But none of us ever again climbed the escapeway to the roof.

About the Author

Borden Deal (1922-   ) ⎯⎯⎯⎯⎯

Borden Deal is one of America's most successful authors. He has written more than a hundred stories, many of which have been adapted for the movies, the stage, television, and radio. His books have been translated into twenty-five languages, and one novel was made into a Broadway musical.

Born in Pontotoc, Mississippi, Deal traveled around the country as a youth, working at a wide variety of jobs. At the age of twenty, he began writing while with the U.S. Department of Labor. He did not publish his first work, however, until six years later, following service in the navy. Today, his short stories are found in dozens of anthologies.

Focus on the Story

The **protagonist** is the hero of the story. The protagonist is usually the main character.

▶ 1. The protagonist of "Antaeus" is _____.
   a. the author
   b. Blackie
   c. T.J.

The **antagonist** is usually the villain of the story—the person who creates a conflict for the main character.

▶ 2. The antagonist of this story is _____.
   a. the man who owned the building
   b. the police
   c. the night watchman

In many stories, the characters change. This is called **character development.** Look back through the story to see how T.J. and his friends changed.

▶ 3. The author said of T.J., "He had planted more than grass. He had planted something important in our minds." How did the boys change as a result of meeting T.J.?
   a. They learned how to speak slowly and gently.
   b. They found out about life in Alabama.
   c. They discovered the joy of planning and accomplishing something important.

A **symbol** is something that represents (stands for) something. For example, *Antaeus* is a symbol of strength. Antaeus was a character in Greek mythology. According to the myth, Antaeus was a giant wrestler who could not be beaten as long as he was touching the earth.

▶ 4. In this story, T.J. symbolizes Antaeus because he _____.
   a. loved the earth and drew strength from it
   b. enjoyed wrestling
   c. was as strong as a giant

Setting

▶ 5. What is the setting of "Antaeus"?
   a. a rooftop
   b. Alabama
   c. a forest

Focus on the Language

Metaphor

▶ **1.** Each of the following sentences describes the grass. Which description is a metaphor?
a. It was a thick carpet over the earth now.
b. It looked rich and black, ready to receive the seed.
c. The patch of greenness stood out above the city surroundings.

A **symbol** may be used as a metaphor.

Example:
• He is a Hercules.

▶ **2.** Which sentence from the story is a metaphor?
a. The gusts of his anger blew among us.
b. It is easier to destroy than to build.
c. He was a new Antaeus, preparing his bed of strength.

Dialect is the local use of language. In different parts of the country, words or phrases may be spoken in different ways.

▶ **3.** T.J. made the following statements. In which sentence does he use dialect?
a. I had my own land for growing cotton.
b. I spent all my life trying *not* to raise grass.
c. I thought you said this was you-all's roof.

Talk It Over

1. Why is this story called "Antaeus"? Would "T.J." have been a better title?
2. Why did the boys destroy the garden on which they had spent so much time? Was this the right thing for them to do?
3. How do you feel about the way the adults acted when they discovered the garden? What else might they have done? Did the boys have any right to use someone else's property?
4. The author said, "It is easier to destroy than to build." What did he mean by this? Do you agree?
5. Why did T.J. run away at the end of the story?

Anne Frank: The Diary of a Young Girl

Most people are never faced with the kind of horror with which Anne Frank lived. Yet, Anne managed to remain hopeful. She shared her hopes and fears with "Kitty," her diary.

Saturday, 20 June, 1942

Dear Kitty,

. . . I haven't written for a few days, because I wanted first of all to think about my diary. It's an odd idea for someone like me to keep a diary; not only because I have never done so before, but because it seems to me that neither I—nor for that matter anyone else—will be interested in . . . a thirteen-year-old girl. Still, what does that matter? I want to write. But more than that, I want to bring out all kinds of things that lie buried deep in my heart. . . .

I don't intend to show this cardboard-covered notebook, bearing the proud name of "diary" to anyone, unless I find a real friend, boy or girl.

Probably nobody cares. And now I come to the root of the matter, the reason for my starting a diary: It is that I have no such real friend.

Let me put it more clearly, since no one will believe that a girl of thirteen feels herself quite alone in the world, nor is it so. I have darling parents and a sister of sixteen. . . . I know about thirty people whom one might call friends. . . . I have relations, aunts and uncles, who are darlings too, a good home. No—I don't seem to lack anything. But it's the same with all my friends, just fun and joking, nothing more. . . . We don't seem to be able to get any closer. . . .

Hence, this diary. . . . I don't want to set down a series of bald facts in a diary like most people do. But I want this diary itself to be my friend. And I shall call my friend Kitty. . . . I will start by sketching in brief the story of my life.

My father was thirty-six when he married my mother, who was then twenty-five. My sister Margot was born in 1926 in Frankfort-on-Main. I followed on June 12, 1929. As we are Jewish, we emigrated to Holland in 1933. . . .

The rest of our family felt the full impact of Hitler's anti-Jewish laws. So life was filled with anxiety. . . . After May 1940, good times rapidly fled. . . . Anti-Jewish decrees followed each other in quick succession. Jews must wear a yellow star. Jews must hand in their bicycles. Jews are forbidden to drive. Jews are only allowed to do their shopping between three and five o'clock and then only in shops which bear the sign "Jewish shop." Jews must be indoors by eight o'clock and cannot even sit in their own gardens after that hour. Jews are forbidden to visit theaters and other places of entertainment. Jews may not take part in public sports. . . .

So we could not do this and were forbidden to do that. But life went on in spite of it all. . . .

So far, everything is all right with the four of us and here I come to the present day.

Sunday morning, 5 July, 1942

Dear Kitty,

Daddy has been at home a lot lately, as there is nothing for him to do at business. . . . A few days ago, Daddy began to talk of us going into hiding. I asked him why on earth he was beginning to talk of that already. "Yes, Anne," he said, "you know that we have been taking food, clothes, furniture to other people for more than a year now. We don't want our belongings to be seized by the Germans. But we certainly don't want to fall into their clutches ourselves. So we shall disappear of our own accord and not wait until they come and fetch us."

"But Daddy, when would it be?" He spoke so seriously that I grew very anxious.

"Don't worry about it. We shall arrange everything. Make the most of your carefree young life while you can." That was all. . . .

Yours, Anne

Wednesday, 8 July, 1942

Dear Kitty,

Years seem to have passed between Sunday and now. So much has happened. It is just as if the whole world has turned upside down. But I am still alive, Kitty, and that is the main thing, Daddy says.

Yes, I'm still alive, indeed. But don't ask where or how. You wouldn't understand a word, so I will begin by telling you what happened on Sunday afternoon.

At three o'clock someone rang the front doorbell. . . . A bit later, Margot appeared at the kitchen door looking very excited. "The SS have sent a call-up notice for Daddy," she whispered. It was a great shock to me, a call-up. Everyone knows what that means. I picture concentration camps and lonely cells—should we allow him to be doomed to this? "Of course he won't go," declared Margot, while we waited together. "Mother has gone to the Van Daans to discuss whether we should move into our hiding place tomorrow. The Van Daans are going with us. So we shall be seven in all. . . ."

Into hiding—where would we go, in a town or the country, in a house or a cottage, when, how, where . . . ?

These were the questions I was not allowed to ask. But I couldn't get them out of my mind. Margot began to pack some of our most vital belongings into a schoolbag. The first thing I put in was this diary. . . . I still didn't know where our secret hiding place was to be. At seven-thirty the door closed. Moortje, my little cat, was the only creature to whom I said farewell. . . .

Yours, Anne

Friday, 10 July, 1942

Dear Kitty,

When we arrived . . . Miep took us quickly upstairs and into the "Secret Annex." She closed the door behind us and we were alone. Margot was already waiting for us, having come faster on her bicycle. . . . All the cardboard boxes which had been sent to the office in the previous months lay piled on the floor and the beds. . . . The whole day long we unpacked boxes, filled cupboards, hammered and tidied, until we were dead beat. We sank into clean beds that night. . . .

Yours, Anne

Saturday, 11 July, 1942

Dear Kitty,

I expect you will be interested to hear what it feels like to "disappear." Well, all I can say is that I don't know myself. . . . The "Secret Annex" is an ideal hiding place. Although it leans to one side and is damp, you'd never find such a comfortable hiding place in Amsterdam. No, perhaps not even in the whole of Holland. Our little room looked very bare at first with nothing on the walls. But thanks to Daddy who had brought my film-star collection and picture postcards . . . I have transformed the walls into one gigantic picture. . . . We have forbidden Margot to cough at night, although she has a bad cold. . . . It is the silence that frightens me so in the evenings and at night. . . . I'm very afraid that we shall be discovered and shot. . . . We have to whisper and tread lightly during the day, otherwise the people in the warehouse might hear us. . . .

Yours, Anne

Wednesday, 13 January, 1943

Dear Kitty,

Everything has upset me again this morning. So I wasn't able to finish a single thing properly.

It is terrible outside. Day and night, people are being dragged off. . . . Families are torn apart. The men, women, and children all become separated. Children coming home from school find that their parents have disappeared. Women return from shopping to find their homes shut up and their families gone.

The Dutch people are anxious too, their sons are being sent to Germany. Everyone is afraid.

And every night hundreds of planes fly over Holland and go to German towns, where the earth is plowed up by their bombs. And every hour hundreds and thousands of people are killed in Russia and Africa. No one is able to keep out of it. The whole globe is waging war. . . . The end is not yet in sight. . . .

Yours, Anne

Wednesday, 3 May, 1944

Dear Kitty,

As you can easily imagine, we often ask ourselves here . . . "What, oh, what is the use of war? Why can't people live peacefully together? Why all this destruction?"

The question is very understandable. But no one has found an answer to it so far. Yes, why do they make still bigger planes, still heavier bombs? Why should millions be spent daily on the war and yet there's not a penny available for medical services, artists, or for poor people?

Why do some people have to starve, while food is rotting in other parts of the world? Oh, why are people so crazy? . . .

Yours, Anne

Saturday, 15 July, 1944

Dear Kitty,

　It's really a wonder that I haven't dropped all my ideals. They seem so absurd and impossible to carry out. Yet I keep them because in spite of everything, I still believe that people are really good at heart. I simply can't build up my hopes on a foundation of confusion, misery, and death. I see the world gradually being turned into a wilderness. I hear the ever approaching thunder, which will destroy us too. I can feel the sufferings of millions. And yet, if I look up into the heavens, I think that it will all come right, that this cruelty too will end, and that peace and tranquillity will return again.

　In the meantime, I must uphold my ideals. Perhaps the time will come when I shall be able to carry them out.

Yours, Anne

About the Author

Anne Frank (1929-1945)

Anne Frank lived with her family in Amsterdam, Holland, during World War II. When the Nazis invaded Holland, the Franks, who were Jewish, were forced to flee to a hiding place in the back of an old warehouse. From this "Secret Annex," as she called it, Anne wrote her diary.

On August 4, 1944, the secret police raided the "Annex." Anne and the other occupants were arrested and sent to concentration camps. In March, 1945, just two months before Holland was liberated, Anne died in the concentration camp at Bergen-Belsen. Her diary was found among a pile of old books in the "Annex" by her father, the only family survivor.

Anne's diary is remarkable—not only for its literary style—but for the courage and insight it offers. It was begun when Anne was only thirteen years old. This true story has touched the hearts of millions of readers around the world.

Focus on the Diary

An autobiography is a type of literature in which a person tells about his or her own life. Autobiographies are classified as nonfiction. They tell about real characters and events.

Protagonist

▶ **1.** The protagonist in "The Diary of a Young Girl" is _____ .
a. Anne Frank
b. Margot Frank
c. Anne's father

Characterization

▶ **2.** Which sentence best describes Anne Frank?
a. She was thoughtless and unfriendly.
b. She was sensitive and hopeful.
c. She was always happy.

Antagonist

▶ **3.** The antagonists in this selection are _____ .

a. Anne's parents
b. the Van Daans
c. the Nazi soldiers

The **author's purpose** is the reason behind his or her writing. The author's purpose is usually to entertain, inform, teach, or convince. But sometimes, an author may have a very personal reason for writing.

▶ **4.** Anne Frank kept a diary because she _____ .

a. hoped many people would read about her
b. wished to share her deepest thoughts with a "friend"
c. wanted to convince people that war was wrong

Focus on the Language

One way of finding the definition of a word is by using the dictionary. Another way is to see how the **word** is used in the sentence, or **in context.**

▷ **1.** Anne Frank was born in Germany. With her parents and sister, she emigrated from Germany to Holland in 1933. The word *emigrated* means _____.

a. moved away
b. wrote to
c. spoke about

2. What is the meaning of the word *tranquillity* in the sentence below?
I believe that this cruelty will end and that peace and tranquillity will return again.
a. war
b. noise
c. calm

3. Anne said, "So life is filled with anxiety." The word *anxiety* means _____.
a. happiness
b. fear
c. ability

Find Out More

An **encyclopedia** is a set of books that gives information about many subjects. The books are arranged alphabetically by subject.

▷ **1.** This diary was written in Holland. To find out about this country, in which volume of the encyclopedia would you look?
a. Volume 1   b. Volume 4   c. Volume 8

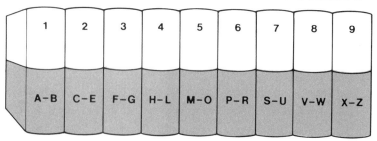

2. To find out more about Anne Frank, look in Volume _____.
a. 1   b. 3   c. 7

Home

Gwendolyn Brooks

---

*"It's going to kill Papa!" she cried out.
"He loves this house! He lives for this
house!"*

What had been wanted was this always, this always to last. The talking softly on this porch with the snake plant in the jardiniere[1] in the southwest corner. The obstinate slip from Aunt Eppie's magnificent Michigan fern at the left side of the friendly door. Mama, Maud Martha, and Helen rocked slowly in their rocking chairs, and looked at the late afternoon light on the lawn and at the emphatic iron of the fence and at the poplar tree. These things might soon be theirs no longer. Those shafts and pools of light, the tree, the graceful iron, might soon be viewed possessively by different eyes.

Papa was to have gone that noon, during his lunch hour, to the office of the Home Owners' Loan. If he had not succeeded in getting another extension, they would be leaving this house in which they had lived for more than fourteen years. There was little hope. The Home Owners' Loan was hard. They sat, making their plans.

"We'll be moving into a nice flat[2] somewhere," said Mama. "Somewhere on South Park, or Michigan, or in Washington Park Court." Those flats, as the girls and Mama knew well, were burdens on wages twice the size of Papa's. This was not mentioned now.

"They're much prettier than this old house," said Helen. "I have friends I'd just as soon not bring here. And I have other friends that wouldn't come down this far for anything, unless they were in a taxi."

[1] *jardiniere:* a pot for plants

[2] *flat:* an apartment

Yesterday, Maud Martha would have attacked her. Tomorrow she might. Today she said nothing. She merely gazed at a little hopping robin in the tree, her tree, and tried to keep the fronts of her eyes dry.

"Well, I do know," said Mama, turning her hands over and over, "that I've been getting tireder and tireder of doing that firing.[3] From October to April, there's firing to be done."

"But lately we've been helping, Harry and I," said Maud Martha. "And sometimes in March and April and in October, and even in November, we could build a little fire in the fireplace. Sometimes the weather was just right for that."

She knew, from the way they looked at her, that this had been a mistake. They did not want to cry.

But she felt that the little line of white, sometimes ridged with smoked purple, and all that cream-shot saffron[4] would never drift across any western sky except that in back of this house. The rain would drum with as sweet a dullness nowhere but here. The birds on South Park were mechanical birds, no better than the poor caught canaries in those "rich" women's sun parlors.

"It's just going to kill Papa!" burst out Maud Martha. "He loves this house! He *lives* for this house!"

"He lives for us," said Helen. "It's us he loves. He wouldn't want the house, except for us."

"And he'll have us," added Mama, "wherever."

"You know," Helen sighed, "if you want to know the truth, this is a re-

[3] *firing:* starting a fire in a coal stove
[4] *saffron:* a yellow-orange color

58

lief. If this hadn't come up, we would have gone on, just dragged on, hanging out here forever."

"It might," allowed Mama, "be an act of God. God may just have reached down and picked up the reins."

"Yes," Maud Martha cracked in, "that's what you always say—that God knows best."

Her mother looked at her quickly, decided the statement was not suspect, looked away.

Helen saw Papa coming. "There's Papa," said Helen.

They could not tell a thing from the way Papa was walking. It was that same dear little staccato walk,[5] one shoulder down, then the other, then repeat, and repeat. They watched his progress. He passed the Kennedys', he passed the vacant lot, he passed

Mrs. Blakemore's. They wanted to hurl themselves over the fence, into the street, and shake the truth out of his collar. He opened his gate—the gate—and still his stride and face told them nothing.

"Hello," he said.

Mama got up and followed him through the front door. The girls knew better than to go in too.

Presently Mama's head emerged. Her eyes were lamps turned on.

"It's all right," she exclaimed. "He got it. It's all over. Everything is all right."

The door slammed shut. Mama's footsteps hurried away.

"I think," said Helen, rocking rapidly, "I think I'll give a party. I haven't given a party since I was eleven. I'd like some of my friends to just casually see that we're homeowners."

---

[5] *staccato walk:* short steps

About the Author

Gwendolyn Brooks (1917-   ) _____

Best known as a writer of poems and short stories, Gwendolyn Brooks began writing as a young child. She stated: "I loved poetry very early and began to put rhymes together at about seven, at which time my parents expressed most earnest confidence that I would one day be a writer. At the age of thirteen my first poem, 'Eventide,' was accepted and printed by a then well-known children's magazine. . . ."

Brooks lectures at universities and colleges throughout the country and has received many awards and prizes for her writing. She won Guggenheim fellowships in 1946 and 1947 and was awarded the Pulitzer Prize in poetry for *Annie Allen* in 1950. She is the book reviewer for the *Chicago Sun-Times.*

"Home" originally appeared in her novel, *Maud Martha.*

Focus on the Story

The **tone** of the story is the overall effect of the writing. For example, the tone may be funny, sad, or suspenseful.

▶ **1.** The tone of "Home" is _____.
a. light and funny
b. serious and quiet
c. terrifying

The **time span** of a story is the time between the beginning and the ending of a story.

▶ **2.** Which best describes the time span of this story?
a. a year
b. a day
c. a week

Motive

▶ **3.** At the conclusion of "Home," Helen decides to give a party because she _____.
a. was having a birthday
b. hadn't had a party since she was eleven
c. was proud to be a homeowner

The **theme** of the story is the main idea. The details in a story help develop the theme.

▶ **4.** Which sentence best expresses the theme of the story?
a. A family is worried about losing its home.
b. A house is not a very important thing to most people.
c. An old house is hard to heat.

Focus on the Language

The repetition of consonant sounds is called **alliteration.**

Examples:
• She *t*old a *t*ale of *t*error.
• They *s*ang *s*ad *s*ongs.

▶ **1.** Which sentence contains alliteration?
a. They looked at the light on the lawn.
b. They did not want to cry.
c. They sat, making their plans.

A **verb** is a word that shows action.

Examples:
- She *said* nothing.
- He *lives* for us.

An **adverb** is a word that describes a verb.

Examples:
- Mother looked at her *quickly*.
- The rain drummed *sweetly*.

Metaphor

Find Out More

Every library has information about the books on its shelves. You can find this information in the **card catalogue.** The card catalogue has three types of cards: *author cards, title cards,* and *subject cards.* This means you can look up a book under the *author's last name,* under its *title,* or under its *subject.* The cards are arranged alphabetically.

▶ **2.** In "Home," Maud Martha said, "We could build a little fire in the fireplace." Which word is a verb?
a. we
b. build
c. little

▶ **3.** Which word in the following sentence is an adverb?
They rocked slowly in their rocking chairs.
a. they
b. slowly
c. rocked

▶ **4.** Which sentence from the story is a metaphor?
a. Her eyes were lamps turned on.
b. There was little hope.
c. The door slammed shut.

▶ **1.** To find more stories by Gwendolyn Brooks, in which drawer of the card catalogue should you look?
a. arl - bas
b. bas - but
c. but - cam

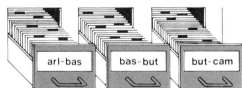

2. To find Gwendolyn Brooks' novel, *Maud Martha,* in which drawer of the card catalogue should you look?
a. lur - mai
b. mai - ned
c. ned - ora

61

DREAMS

Langston Hughes

Hold fast to dreams
For if dreams die
Life is a broken-winged bird
That cannot fly.

Hold fast to dreams
For when dreams go
Life is a barren field
Frozen with snow.

HARLEM

Langston Hughes

What happens to a dream deferred?

Does it dry up
like a raisin in the sun?
Or fester like a sore—
And then run?
Does it stink like rotten meat?
Or crust and sugar over—
like a syrupy sweet?

Maybe it just sags
like a heavy load.

Or does it explode?

Focus on the Poems

Metaphor

▶ **1.** Which line in the first stanza of "Dreams" is a metaphor?
a. Hold fast to dreams
b. For if dreams die
c. Life is a broken-winged bird

2. According to Langston Hughes, what does life become when dreams go?
a. a barren field
b. a frozen lake
c. a nightmare

Simile

▶ **3.** In "Harlem," Hughes begins the poem with a question. He answers this question by asking more questions. Which question does *not* contain a simile?
a. Does it dry up like a raisin in the sun?
b. Does it stink like rotten meat?
c. Or does it explode?

Rhyme

▶ **4.** In "Dreams" which words rhyme?
a. *die* and *fly; go* and *snow*
b. *dreams* and *bird; field* and *frozen*
c. *broken* and *cannot; barren* and *life*

Stanza

▶ **5.** How many stanzas are there in the poem, "Dreams"?
a. one
b. two
c. three

Unit Review

Write your answers on a separate sheet of paper.

1. The antagonist in a story creates a conflict for the _____.
   - **a.** theme
   - **b.** stanza
   - **c.** protagonist

2. Which statement is true of "Antaeus"?
   - **a.** It is a work of fiction.
   - **b.** It is an autobiography.
   - **c.** It is classified as nonfiction.

3. In "Home," the author's purpose was to _____.
   - **a.** write a humorous story
   - **b.** show how a family reacts to the possibility that it will lose its home
   - **c.** prove that people don't care about where they live

4. The time span of "Diary of a Young Girl" is _____.
   - **a.** a few weeks
   - **b.** several months
   - **c.** years

5. The theme of "Dreams" is that _____.
   - **a.** one should not hope for too much
   - **b.** dreams are important to life
   - **c.** life is filled with troubles

6. Match each term with its definition.
   - **a.** tone — something that stands for, or represents, something else __
   - **b.** symbol — the changes in a character during the course of the story __
   - **c.** character development — the overall effect of the writing __

Reviewing the Language

1. T.J. made the following statements. In which one is there an example of dialect?
   a. We could make our own field right here.
   b. I fed my acre of corn to my calf.
   c. You get part of the bale offen your acre.

2. In "Antaeus," the boys prepared the rich, black earth. In this sentence, the word *prepared* is a(n) _____ .
   a. adjective
   b. adverb
   c. verb

3. Which sentence contains an example of alliteration?
   a. Mama's footsteps hurried away.
   b. Everything is all right.
   c. Helen sat rocking rapidly.

4. What is the meaning of the word *forbidden* in the following sentence from "Diary of a Young Girl"?
   Jews are *forbidden* to visit theaters and other places of entertainment.
   a. allowed
   b. not allowed
   c. asked

Talking It Over

1. In each story in this unit, characters "held onto a dream." Think about T.J., Anne Frank, and the family in "Home." What dreams did these characters have? How did they try to hold onto their dreams?

2. Which stories deal with a question of injustice? Which stories are likely to make readers think about things that they may have taken for granted?

3. Which character in this unit did you like or respect the most? Who was the most courageous? Who succeeded in seeing a dream come true?

4. According to Langston Hughes, why should a person "hold fast to dreams"? What happens to "a dream deferred"?

5. What is the difference between "dreams" and "daydreams"?

Unit 3

Facing Death

Death is always new.

—West African Proverb

A Day's Wait

Ernest Hemingway

The boy was staring at the foot of the bed. "About what time do you think I'm going to die?" he asked.

He came into the room to shut the windows while we were still in bed. I saw he looked ill. He was shivering. His face was white. He walked slowly as though it hurt to move.

"What's the matter, Schatz?"

"I've got a headache."

"You better go back to bed."

"No, I'm all right."

"You go to bed. I'll see you when I'm dressed."

But when I came downstairs, he was dressed. He sat by the fire, looking a very sick and unhappy boy of nine years. When I put my hand on his forehead, I knew he had a fever.

"You go up to bed," I said, "You're sick."

"I'm all right," he said.

When the doctor came, he took the boy's temperature.

"What is it?" I asked him.

"One hundred and two."

Downstairs, the doctor left three different medicines in different colored capsules. The doctor left instructions for giving them. One was to bring down the fever, another a purgative. The third was to overcome an acid condition. The germs of influenza can only exist in an acid condition, he explained. He seemed to know all about influenza. He said there was nothing to worry about if the fever did not go above one hundred and four degrees. This was a light epidemic of flu. There was no danger as long as you didn't get pneumonia.

Back in the room, I wrote the boy's temperature down and I made a note of the time to give the capsules.

"Do you want me to read to you?"

"All right. If you want to," said the boy. His face was very white. There were dark areas under his eyes. He lay still in the bed. He seemed very detached from what was going on.

I read aloud from Howard Pyle's *Book of Pirates.* But I could see he was not following what I was reading.

"How do you feel, Schatz?" I asked.

"Just the same, so far," he said.

I sat at the foot of the bed. I read to myself while I waited for it to be time to give another capsule. It would have been natural for him to go to sleep. But when I looked up, he was looking at the foot of the bed, looking very strange.

"Why don't you try to go to sleep? I'll wake you up for the medicine."

"I'd rather stay awake."

After a while he said to me, "You don't have to stay in here with me, Papa, if it bothers you."

"It doesn't bother me."

"No, I mean you don't have to stay if it's going to bother you."

I thought perhaps he was a little lightheaded. After giving him the prescribed capsules at eleven o'clock, I went out for a while.

It was a bright, cold day, the ground covered with a sleet that had frozen. It seemed as if all the bare trees and all the grass and the bare ground had been varnished with ice. I took the young Irish setter for a little walk up the road. But it was difficult to stand or walk on the glassy surface. The red dog slipped and I fell twice.

At the house they said the boy had refused to let anyone into the room.

"You can't come in," he said. "You musn't get what I have."

I went up to him and found him in exactly the position I had left him. He was white-faced but with the tops of his cheeks flushed by the fever. He was staring still, as he had stared, at the foot of the bed.

I took his temperature.

"What is it?"

"Something like a hundred," I said. It was one hundred and two and four tenths.

"It was a hundred and two," he said.

"Who said so?"

"The doctor."

"Your temperature is all right,' I said. "It's nothing to worry about."

"I don't worry," he said. "But I can't keep from thinking."

"Don't think," I said. "Just take it easy."

"I'm taking it easy," he said and looked straight ahead. He was evidently holding tight on to himself about something.

"Take this with water."

"Do you think it will do any good?"

"Of course it will."

I sat down and opened the *Pirate* book and began to read, but I could see he was not following, so I stopped.

"About what time do you think I'm going to die?" he asked.

"What?"

"About how long will it be before I die?"

"You aren't going to die. What's the matter with you?"

"Oh, yes, I am. I heard him say a hundred and two."

"People don't die with a fever of one hundred and two. That's a silly way to talk."

"I know they do. At school in France the boys told me you can't live with forty-four degrees. I've got a hundred and two."

He had been waiting to die all day, ever since nine o'clock in the morning.

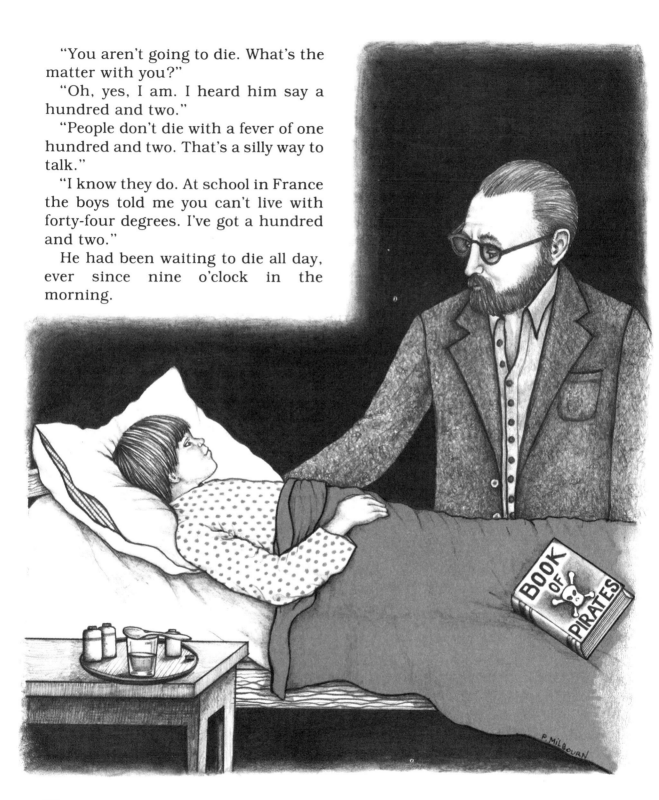

"You poor Schatz," I said. "Poor old Schatz. It's like miles and kilometers. You aren't going to die. That's a different thermometer. On that thermometer, thirty-seven is normal. On this kind, it's ninety-eight."

"Are you sure?"

"Absolutely," I said. "It's like miles and kilometers. You know. Like how many kilometers we make when we do seventy miles in the car?"

"Oh," he said.

But his gaze at the foot of the bed relaxed slowly. The hold over himself relaxed too, finally. The next day it was very slack and he cried very easily at little things that were of no importance.

About the Author

Ernest Hemingway (1899-1961) —————

Ernest Hemingway is one of the most famous of modern American authors. His crisp, strong style of writing and his concern with courage and honor have influenced many other writers.

Hemingway was born in Oak Park, Illinois. He later lived in France, Africa, and Spain. His experiences as a boxer, big game hunter, and war correspondent helped provide the subject matter for much of his work.

Among Hemingway's best-known novels are *A Farewell to Arms, The Sun Also Rises, For Whom the Bell Tolls,* and *The Old Man and the Sea.* In 1954, he received the Nobel prize for literature.

A colorful man, who lived a life filled with danger and adventure, Hemingway committed suicide in 1961, after a serious illness.

Focus on the Story

The person who tells the story is known as the **narrator.** Often, the narrator is one of the characters in the story.

▶ **1.** The narrator of "A Day's Wait" is _____ .
   a. Schatz
   b. the doctor
   c. the father

Stories are told from a *first-person* or a *third-person* **point of view.** In the first person point of view, a character tells the story, using the words, *I* or *me.* In the third-person point of view, the author—acting as an observer—tells the story, using the words *he, she,* or *they.*

▶ **2.** "A Day's Wait" is told _____ .
   a. from a first-person point of view
   b. from a third-person point of view
   c. by a character not in the story

Author's Style

▶ **3.** Which of the following is true of Hemingway's style of writing?
   a. He writes many short lines of dialogue.
   b. He never uses verbs.
   c. He uses rhyme in most of his work.

Author's Purpose

▶ **4.** Which of the following best describes the author's purpose for writing "A Day's Wait"?
   a. to inform the reader
   b. to convince the reader
   c. to entertain the reader

Setting

▶ **5.** The setting of this story is _____ .
   a. a house
   b. a schoolroom
   c. a hospital

Focus on the Language

Synonyms are words that have the same or very similar meanings.

Examples:
- *Toss* is a synonym for *throw.*
- *Automobile* is a synonym for *car.*

Antonyms are words that have opposite meanings.

Examples:
- *Sharp* is an antonym for *dull.*
- *Sweet* is an antonym for *sour.*

Homonyms are words that sound the same but are spelled differently and have different meanings.

Examples:
- *Steal* and *steel* are homonyms.
- *Horse* and *hoarse* are homonyms.

▶ **1.** In "A Day's Wait," Schatz had a fever and was shivering. A synonym for *shivering* is _____ .

a. *angry*
b. *shaking*
c. *pale*

▶ **2.** While his father read him a book, Schatz "seemed very detached from what was going on." An antonym for *detached* is _____ .
a. *interested*
b. *bored*
c. *happy*

▶ **3.** The title of this story is "A Day's Wait." A homonym for *wait* is _____ .
a. *stay*
b. *go*
c. *weight*

Write About It

Look at the selection below. Choose the word that correctly completes each sentence. On a separate sheet of paper, rewrite the paragraph.

"A Day's Wait" is the story of a (man, boy, doctor) named Schatz. This character was (wealthy, happy, ill). From his bed, he asked his father, "About what time do you think I'm going to (work, leave, die)?"

The father said, "That's a (smart, silly, amusing) way to talk. The boy had a (grandfather, pulse, temperature) of one hundred and two. He thought he was (dying, rich, old). He didn't know there are two kinds of (thermometers, miles, kilometers). On one, ninety-eight degrees is (normal, dangerous, accurate). He had been waiting to die all (week, night, day).

The Story of an Hour

Kate Chopin

There was something coming to her.
She was waiting for it, fearfully.
What was it? She did not know. But
she felt it creeping out of the sky.

Knowing that Mrs. Mallard had heart trouble, great care was taken to break the news of her husband's death. It was her sister, Josephine, who told her gently. Her husband's friend, Richards, was there, too. He had been in the newspaper office when word of the railroad accident was received. Brently Mallard's name headed the list of those "killed."

Richards quickly checked its truth by sending a second telegram. Then he hurried to deliver the sad message.

Mrs. Mallard immediately understood what had happened. She wept at once, wildly, in her sister's arms. When the storm of grief had passed, she went to her room alone. She would let no one follow her.

Facing the open window stood a large armchair. Into this she sank, pressed down by a weariness that haunted her body and seemed to reach into her soul.

In the open square before her house, she saw the tops of trees. They were fluttering with new spring life. The sweet smell of rain was in the air. In the street below, she heard a peddler shouting. The notes of a distant song reached her ears. And countless sparrows were twittering on the roof.

Patches of blue sky showed here and there. They burst through the clouds that piled, one above the other, in the west facing her window.

She sat with her head thrown back on the chair. She did not move, except when a sob came up into her throat and shook her.

She was young, with a fair, calm face, whose lines showed a certain strength. But now, there was a dull stare in her eyes. She was gazing at one of those patches of blue sky.

There was something coming to her. She was waiting for it, fearfully. What was it? She did not know. But she felt it, creeping out of the sky. It was reaching toward her through the sound, the smells, the color that filled the air.

Her heart began to pound wildly. She was beginning to recognize this thing that was approaching her. She was trying to beat it back with her will. But she was powerless to do so.

When she let herself go, a whispered word escaped from her slightly parted lips. She said it over and over under her breath. "Free, free, *free!*"

The empty stare, and the look of terror that had followed it, left her eyes. They stayed sharp and bright. Her pulse beat fast. Pounding blood warmed and relaxed every inch of her body.

Was it a terrible joy that held her? She did not stop to ask. The question did not seem important.

She knew that she would weep again when she saw her husband's kind and tender hands folded in death. He had never looked at her except with love. But she saw beyond that bitter moment. She saw the long years to come—years that would belong to her completely. And she opened and spread her arms out to them in welcome.

There would be no one to live for during those coming years. She would live for herself!

And yet she had loved him—sometimes. Often, she had not. What did it matter! What could love, the unsolved mystery, count for in the face of this emotion, this sudden sense of freedom.

"Free! Body and soul free!" she kept whispering.

Josephine was kneeling before the closed door. She had her mouth to the keyhole, crying to be let in. "Louise, open the door! I beg! Open the door! You will make yourself ill. What are you doing. Louise? For heaven's sake, open the door."

"Go away. I am not making myself ill." No, she was drinking in life itself through that open window.

Her thoughts were running wildly to those days ahead of her. Spring days, and summer days, and all sorts of days that would be her own. She breathed a quick prayer that life might be long. It was only yesterday she had thought with a chill that life might be long.

She arose finally and opened the door. There was triumph in her eyes, and she carried herself like a goddess of Victory. She put her arm around her sister, and together they went down the stairs. Richards stood waiting for them at the bottom.

Someone was opening the front door with a key. It was Brently Mallard who entered, calmly carrying his suitcase and umbrella. He had been far from the scene of the accident, and did not even know there had been one. He stood amazed at Josephine's loud cry, at Richards' quick motion to screen him from the view of his wife.

But Richards was too late.

When the doctors came, they said she had died of a heart attack—of joy that kills.

About the Author

Kate Chopin (1851-1904) _____

Born in St. Louis, Kate Chopin moved to Louisiana after her marriage in 1870. She lived there for the next ten years and grew to know and love New Orleans, the setting of many of her stories. Following her husband's death in 1883, Chopin began to write professionally.

Chopin's work usually deals with the difficulties involved in love and marriage. She was very concerned with human relationships and was a strong supporter of equality between men and women. Chopin is best known for her novel, *The Awakening*.

Focus on the Story

Main Character

▶ **1.** The main character in "The Story of an Hour" is _____.
a. Louise Mallard
b. Brently Mallard
c. Richards

Character Development

▶ **2.** During the course of the story, Mrs. Mallard allowed herself to experience a powerful emotion. What was it?
a. a feeling of terror
b. a sense of freedom
c. jealousy towards her sister

The **climax** of a story is its turning point. In most stories, the climax is the event which causes a character to take some important action.

▶ **3.** The climax of the story was the moment when _____.
a. Mrs. Mallard opened the door for her sister
b. Brently Mallard appeared
c. Richards received word of the train accident

Irony is when something happens in a story which is the opposite of what is expected. Such a situation is said to be ironic.

▶ **4.** It was ironic that Mrs. Mallard _____.
a. wanted to be alone in her grief
b. loved her husband
c. died just when life was beginning to have meaning for her

Narrator

▶ **5.** The narrator of this story is _____.
a. Louise Mallard
b. Brently Mallard
c. not a character in the story

Focus on the Language

▶ **Concrete words** name things that can be touched, heard, smelled, seen, or tasted.

Examples:
  • sky
  • flower

Abstract words name ideas that *cannot* be touched, heard, smelled, seen, or tasted.

Examples:
  • friendship
  • jealousy
  • hate

Adverb

▶ **1.** Which of the following is a concrete word?
a. telegram
b. freedom
c. triumph

▶ **2.** To describe Mrs. Mallard's feelings, the author used abstract words. Which group below contains abstract words?
a. chair, clouds, sister
b. freedom, joy, love
c. suitcase, umbrella, message

▶ **3.** Which word in the following sentence is an adverb?
Her thoughts ran wildly.
a. thoughts
b. ran
c. wildly

Find Out More

The **dictionary** is a reference book which gives information about the correct meaning, spelling, and pronunciation of words. Entries in a dictionary are placed in alphabetical order.

▶ **1.** When Mrs. Mallard saw her husband at the door, she was astounded. Look up the definition of the word *astounded* in the dictionary. The correct meaning is _____.
a. pleased
b. saddened
c. amazed

2. Mrs. Mallard's fate might be considered *tragic*. Look up the definition of the word *tragic* in the dictionary. The correct meaning is _____.
a. deserved
b. very sad
c. unusual

An Occurrence at Owl Creek Bridge

Ambrose Bierce

"If I could free my hands," he thought, "I might pull off the noose and jump into the stream. I could swim to the shore, run into the woods, and get away home."

Part I

A man stood on a bridge in northern Alabama. He was looking down into the swift water twenty feet below. The man's hands were behind his back, and his wrists were tied with a cord. A rope was around his neck. It was attached to a large piece of wood above his head.

The man was standing on a wooden platform. It had been specially made for this purpose. Near him were the men who were going to hang him. They were soldiers of the Union army. A short distance away was an armed officer. He was a captain. At each end of the bridge stood a guard with a rifle.

The man who was going to be hanged was about thirty-five years of age. He was not wearing a uniform. Judging from his clothes, he was fairly well-to-do. He was very good looking. His long black hair was combed straight back and fell behind his ears. He had a mustache and a pointed beard. His large dark gray eyes had a kindly expression. Clearly, this was no common killer.

Everything now appeared to be ready. The two privates stepped back. The sergeant turned to the captain and saluted. The sergeant was waiting for the signal.

The condemned man looked at the water below. He saw a piece of wood bobbing up and down. His followed it

79

down the stream. How slowly it seemed to move! What a lazy stream!

He closed his eyes in order to fix his last thoughts upon his wife and children. The water, sparkling like gold in the early sun, had bothered him. And now, something new began to annoy him. As he thought of his loved ones, he heard a noise. It was a sound he could neither ignore nor understand. It was a sharp, clear sound, like the pounding of a hammer. It kept ringing in his ears. He wondered what it was, and whether it was far away or near—for it seemed to be both. The sounds came again and again. They grew stronger and louder. They hurt his ears like the blows of a knife. He was afraid he would scream.

What he heard was the ticking of his watch.

He opened his eyes and again saw the water below him. "If I could free my hands," he thought, "I might pull off the noose and jump into the stream. By diving under the water, I could avoid the bullets. I could swim to the shore, run into the woods, and get away home. My home, thank goodness, is still outside their lines. My wife and children are still far away from the enemy."

Those were the thoughts that flashed into the brain of the doomed man. At that moment, *the captain gave the signal.*

Part II

Peyton Farquhar was a wealthy farmer. He came from an old and well-known Alabama family. He believed very strongly in the cause of the South. Certain things had kept him from joining the army. But he was a soldier at heart, and he longed to fight. He felt that his time would come. Then he would meet any danger to serve the South.

One evening, Farquhar and his wife were sitting on a bench near the entrance to his land. Just then, a soldier dressed in gray rode up to the gate and asked for a drink of water. Mrs. Farquhar was only too happy to serve him. While she was getting the water, her husband went up to the dusty horseman and asked eagerly for news from the front.

"The Yanks are getting ready to march again," he said. "They have reached the Owl Creek bridge. They have repaired the bridge and plan to

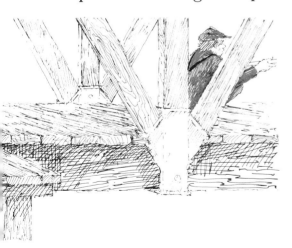

bring supplies over on it. The Union commander has issued an order which is posted everywhere. It says that anyone caught interfering with the bridge will be hanged. I saw the order myself."

"How far is it to the bridge?" asked Farquhar.

"About thirty miles."

"Is there a force on this side of the bridge?"

"Only a small squad about half a mile out. And there's a single guard at this end of the bridge."

"Suppose a man could get around the squad? Suppose he could overpower the guard," said Farquhar, smiling, "what could he do?"

The soldier thought for a moment. "I was there a month ago," he answered. "I remember that last winter's flood threw a great deal of driftwood against the wooden pier at this end of the bridge. It is now dry and would burn like straw."

Mrs. Farquhar brought the water. The soldier drank it and thanked her politely. Then he bowed and rode away. He headed in the direction from which he had come. He was a spy—*for the North!*

Part III

As Peyton Farquhar fell straight down from the bridge, he blacked out and was as one already dead. He was awakened from this state—ages later, it seemed to him—by a sharp pain in his throat. He also felt as though he was choking. Pain shot down his neck to every part of his body.

He became aware that he was falling. Then, all at once, the light about him shot upward. There was the noise of a great splash. There was a sudden roar in his ears, and all was cold and dark. Suddenly, he could think again. He knew that the rope had broken and that he had fallen into the stream.

The noose around his neck was choking him. But at least it kept the water from his lungs. To die of hanging at the bottom of a river! The idea seemed crazy to him. He opened his eyes in the darkness and saw above him a gleam of light. But how far away it seemed!

He was still sinking, for the light became fainter and fainter. Then it began to grow brighter, and he knew he was rising to the surface. There the soldiers would see him. "To be hanged and drowned," he thought, "that is not so bad. But I do not wish to be shot. No, I will not be shot. That is not fair."

There was a sharp pain in his wrists as he tried to free his hands. He tried again. The cords fell away. His arms parted and floated upward. He could see his hands in the growing light. They were grabbing wildly at the noose on his neck. They tore the rope off!

And now he was hit by a blinding pain. His neck ached horribly; his brain was on fire. His heart felt as though it was going to burst. His hands beat the water with quick strokes. They were forcing him to the surface. He felt his head come up out of the water. His eyes were blinded by the sunlight. His lungs filled with air as he took the deepest breath he had ever taken.

He was now in control of himself. He felt the ripples on his face. He heard their sounds as they splashed around his ears. He looked at the forest on the bank of the stream. He saw the trees—saw them clearly—the leaves and the insects on them. He saw flies and gray spiders stretching their webs from twig to twig. He saw rainbow-colored dewdrops on a million blades of grass. A fish slid along beneath his eyes. He heard the rush of its body parting the water.

He turned his head and saw the bridge. He saw the captain, the sergeant, and the two privates. He could see their shadows against the blue sky. They shouted and pointed at him. The captain had drawn his pistol, but he did not fire.

Suddenly he heard a sharp cracking sound. Something struck the water a few inches from his head. He heard a second shot. He saw one of the guards with his rifle at his shoulder. A light cloud of blue smoke was rising from the gun. Farquhar saw the eye of the guard looking at him through the sights of the rifle. He saw that it was a gray eye. He remembered having read that gray eyes were sharpest—that all famous sharpshooters had them.

A current caught Farquhar. It turned him half around. He was now looking at the forest, away from the bridge. A clear, high, singsong voice rang out from behind him. His body turned cold, as he heard the command: "Attention company! Ready . . . Aim . . . *Fire!*"

Farquhar dived—dived as deeply as he could. The water roared like thunder in his ears. He could hear the dull sound of shots. Shining bits of metal touched him on the face and the hands, then fell away. One landed between his collar and his neck. Reaching up, he pulled it out.

He rose to the surface, gasping for air. He had been under water a long time. He was much further downstream and nearer to safety. The soldiers had almost finished reloading. Their rifles shone in the sunshine. The two guards fired again, without hitting him.

The hunted man saw all this over his shoulder. He was now swimming strongly with the current. Suddenly, he felt himself being turned around and around. He was spinning like a top. The water, the forest, the faraway bridge all flew by his eyes. He was thrown upon the shore. He could not believe it! He was safe from his enemies! He dug his fingers into the sand. He threw it over himself in handfuls. He shouted with joy! He wept with delight!

He would have liked to stay there and rest. Shots in the branches above his head quickly changed his mind.

He jumped to his feet and rushed into the forest.

All that day, he traveled. The forest seemed to go on forever. Nowhere did he find a break in it. He had not known that he lived in so wild a place. There was something strange in the discovery.

By nightfall, he was tired, aching and hungry. But the thought of his wife and children urged him on. At last, he found a road which he knew led in the right direction. It was as wide and as straight as a city street. Yet no one was on it.

His neck was in pain. Lifting his hand to it, he found it badly swollen. He knew there must be a circle of black where the rope had bruised it. His eyes felt so large he could no longer close them. His tongue was hot with thirst. He opened his mouth to let in some air. How soft the grass was on the path. He could no longer feel the road beneath his feet! Probably, even though he was suffering, he had fallen asleep while walking.

Part IV

Now he sees another scene. He stands at the gate of his own home. All is just as he left it—bright and beautiful in the morning sunshine. He must have traveled the entire night. He pushes open the gate and passes up the wide white walk. He sees a flutter of female clothing. His wife, looking fresh and cool and sweet comes down from the porch to meet

him. At the bottom of the steps, she stands waiting. Her face is smiling and filled with joy. Ah, how beautiful she is! He rushes forward with arms held out. As he is about to hug her, he feels a stunning blow upon the back of his neck. A blinding white light blazes all about him. There is a sound like the boom of a cannon. Then all is darkness and silence!

Peyton Farquhar was dead. His body, with a broken neck, swung gently from side to side beneath the timbers of the Owl Creek bridge.

About the Author

Ambrose Bierce (1842-1914) _____

Ambrose Bierce was born in a log cabin in Meiggs County, Ohio. After serving in the Civil War, where he was promoted to major, Bierce went to San Francisco to work as a reporter. His first stories were published while he was living in London from 1872-1876. Bierce later returned to California where he spent more than twenty years working on newpapers and writing short stories and articles. In November 1913, Bierce left San Francisco for Mexico, where he disappeared. It is now believed that he was shot during the revolution there.

Bierce's stories often deal with the gruesome or supernatural. Many are shocking and have horrifying surprise endings. His stories about the Civil War are known for their realism and power. The best of Bierce's stories are collected in _Tales of Soldiers and Civilians_ in which "An Occurrence at Owl Creek Bridge" appeared.

Focus on the Story

Setting

▶ **1.** What is the setting of the story?
a. a large house
b. a battlefield during the Civil War
c. a bridge in Alabama

Time Span

▶ **2.** The main action of "An Occurrence at Owl Creek Bridge" takes place over _____.
a. a few seconds
b. a year
c. a month

Motive

▶ **3.** The soldiers hanged Farquhar because he was _____.

a. a spy
b. planning to burn the bridge
c. a member of the Union army

Sometimes a story is interrupted to show events that happened earlier. These events are known as **flashbacks.**

▶ **4.** Which part of this story is told through a flashback?
a. Part I
b. Part II
c. Part III

Protagonist

▶ **5.** The protagonist of this story is _____.
a. Peyton Farquhar
b. the spy from the North
c. the Union captain

Focus on the Language

Simile

▶ **1.** Following are three descriptive statements from the story. Which one contains a simile?

    a. His long black hair was combed straight back and fell behind his ears.

    b. He saw rainbow-colored dewdrops on a million blades of grass.

    c. The water, sparkling like gold in the early sun, had bothered him.

Onomatopoeia

▶ **2.** Which words illustrate onomatopoeia?

    a. bridge, uniform, spy

    b. face, water, soldier

    c. boom, splash, pounding

When figurative language is used too often, it loses its power. An overused simile or metaphor is called a **cliché.**

Examples:
  • quick as a flash
  • hard as a rock

▶ **3.** Which sentence contains an expression which is a cliché?

    a. The captain had drawn his pistol.

    b. He was spinning like a top.

    c. A light cloud of blue smoke was rising.

Talk it Over

1. Most of the action in "An Occurrence at Owl Creek Bridge" takes place in the mind of Peyton Farquhar. Farquhar faced death by imagining that he had escaped. How did this "dream" make Farquhar's death easier for him?

2. What was your reaction to the last two sentences of the story? How does the description of Farquhar's wife in the previous paragraph make his death seem all the more tragic?

3. Were you disappointed to discover that Farquhar had not escaped after all?

4. It is often said that, at the moment of death, a person's life "flashes before his eyes." How does this statement relate to "An Occurrence at Owl Creek Bridge"?

An Appointment in Samarra

W. Somerset Maugham

DEATH SPEAKS:

There was a merchant in Bagdad who sent his servant to market to buy provisions. In a little while, the servant came back, white and trembling. He said, Master, just now when I was in the marketplace, I was jostled by a woman in the crowd. When I turned, I saw it was Death that jostled me. She looked at me and made a threatening gesture. Now, lend me your horse. I will ride away from this city and avoid my fate. I will go to Samarra, and there Death will not find me. The merchant lent him his horse. The servant mounted it. He dug his spurs in its flanks. As fast as the horse could gallop, he went. Then the merchant went down to the marketplace. He saw me standing in the crowd and he came to me and said, Why did you make a threatening gesture to my servant when you saw him this morning? That was not a threatening gesture, I said. It was only a start of surprise. I was astonished to see him in Bagdad, for I had an appointment with him tonight in Samarra.

Focus on the Parable

**A parable is a very short story which is meant to illustrate a
truth or teach a lesson.**

Personification

▶ 1. In this parable, what is personified?
a. the marketplace
b. the servant
c. Death

Irony

▶ 2. The irony in this parable is that _____.
a. the servant fled to Samarra to avoid Death, but
Death was planning to meet him there
b. both the servant and the Master met Death in the
same place
c. Death went to the marketplace in Bagdad

The lesson taught in a parable is
called the **moral.**

▶ 3. What is the moral of this parable?
a. A person can hide from Death by running fast
enough.
b. No one can escape Death.
c. Death does not come by surprise.

Compound words are words that are
made by combining two words to
form a new word.

Examples:
 • *School* and *house* become
 schoolhouse.
 • *In* and *side* become *inside.*

▶ 4. Which word below is a compound word?
a. provisions
b. marketplace
c. threatening

Antagonist

▶ 5. The antagonist in this parable is _____.
a. the merchant
b. the servant
c. Death

Unit Review

Write your answers on a separate sheet of paper.

1. "The Story of an Hour" is told _____.
   a. from a first-person point of view
   b. from a third-person point of view
   c. by a character in the story

2. The person who tells a story is the _____.
   a. main character
   b. flashback
   c. narrator

3. When an event in a story is the opposite of what is expected, it is _____.
   a. ironic
   b. symbolic
   c. a cliché

4. Match each term with its definition.
   a. author's purpose   the turning point of the story ___
   b. setting   where and when the story takes place ___
   c. climax   the reason behind the author's writing ___

5. "An Occurrence at Owl Creek Bridge" is a _____.
   a. short story
   b. parable
   c. work of nonfiction

Reviewing the Language

1. In "An Occurrence at Owl Creek Bridge," Peyton Farquhar was a condemned man. Which word is a synonym for *condemned*?
   a. *happy*
   b. *innocent*
   c. *convicted*

89

2. Mrs. Mallard had a "fair, calm face, whose lines showed a certain strength." An antonym for *strength* is _____ .

    a. *power*
    b. *weakness*
    c. *age*

---

3. Which group of words from "The Story of an Hour" contains compound words?

    a. newspaper, railroad, armchair
    b. immediately, sparrows, weariness
    c. telegram, office, peddler

---

4. When an expression loses its power through overuse, it is called _____ .

    a. a homonym
    b. an abstract word
    c. a cliché

Talking It Over

1. In each story in this unit, a character faced death. Think about Schatz in "A Day's Wait" and the servant in "An Appointment in Samarra." How did each face death differently? How did her husband's death affect Mrs. Mallard? What happened to Peyton Farquhar at the moment of death?

2. In "The Story of an Hour," the doctors said that Mrs. Mallard died "of joy that kills." What did they mean by this? What do *you* think caused Mrs. Mallard's death?

3. "Death is always new" is an old West African saying. How can death be "new"?

About the Poets

ROBERT FROST (1874-1963)

Frost is known as the poet of New England. His early years were not easy. He had to support himself as a teacher and a farmer. To publish his first book of poetry, he spent his own savings. From the moment *A Boy's Will* appeared in 1913, however, Frost was an "immediate success." Over his long career, Frost won the Pulitzer Prize four times. "Stopping by Woods on a Snowy Evening" is one of Frost's best-known poems.

LANGSTON HUGHES (1902-1967)

Hughes was born in Joplin, Missouri. In 1926 after publishing "The Weary Blues" he received a scholarship to Lincoln University in Pennsylvania. In 1935, Hughes won a Guggenheim Fellowship, and in 1947, an American Academy of Arts and Letters Grant. During his career, Hughes wrote poems, songs, short stories, novels, movie scripts, and an autobiography. In all, he published over 50 books. His purpose, he said, always remained the same. It was "to explain and illuminate the Negro condition in America." Langston Hughes was often called "the poet laureate of Harlem." Today, he is recognized as one of the leading American poets of the century.

W. SOMERSET MAUGHAM (1874-1965)

One of the most popular of modern British authors, Maugham wrote numerous short stories, many plays, and a number of novels. His most famous work is *Of Human Bondage,* a realistic novel about a lame medical student. (Maugham himself had become a doctor to please his family, but he never practiced medicine.) Another well-known novel, *The Moon and Sixpence,* is based on the life of the painter Paul Gauguin.

Glossary

Abstract Words–words that name ideas that cannot be touched, heard, smelled, seen, or tasted; for example, *love* and *freedom*

Adjective–a word that describes a **noun;** for example, *lost* dog, *pretty* face

Adverb–a word that describes a **verb;** for example, *quietly* sang, look *carefully*

Alliteration–the repetition of consonant sounds; for example, The *w*ind *w*ailed.

Antagonist–the villain of the story—the person who creates the **conflict** for the main character

Antonyms–words that are opposite in meaning; for example, *up* is an antonym for *down*.

Author's Purpose–the reason the author wrote the story. An author's purpose may be to entertain, inform, teach, or convince.

Author's Style–the way an author uses words; the arrangement of words and sentences

Autobiography–a type of literature in which a person tells about his or her own life. Autobiographies are classified as **nonfiction.**

Card Catalogue–an alphabetically arranged index file which gives information about library books

Character–a person in the story

Character Development–the change in a character from the beginning to the ending of a story

Characterization–ways of showing what a character is like. The way a character looks, talks, acts, or thinks is part of his or her characterization.

Cliché–figurative language that has lost its power because of overuse; for example, *He was green with envy.*

Climax–the turning point of the story

Compound Word–a word formed by combining two or more words; for example, *table* and *cloth* become *tablecloth.*

Concrete Words–words that name things that can be touched, heard, smelled, seen, or tasted; for example, *siren, apple, boat*

Conflict–a fight or difference of opinion. In a story, there can be a conflict between characters, a conflict between a character and nature, or a conflict in the mind of a character. (See **inner conflict.**)

Dialect–the local use of language. In different parts of the country, the choice of words, how they are used, and how they are spoken can be different.

Dialogue–the speech between characters in a story

Dictionary–a book that lists words alphabetically and includes the meaning of each word

Episode–an event in a story; a part of the **plot**

Fiction–a story that is made up or imagined

Figurative Language–descriptive language which is not meant to be taken literally. For example, *It's raining cats and dogs.* (**Metaphors, similes,** and **personification** are also examples of figurative language.)

Flashback–an interruption in a story in which events that happened earlier are told

Foreshadowing–clues in a story that help the reader guess what will happen next

Homonyms–words that sound the same but are spelled differently and have different meanings; for example, *wait* is a homonym for *weight.*

Imagery–the picture the writer creates in the mind of the reader

Inner Conflict–a conflict in the mind of a character

Irony–when something happens which is the opposite of what is expected

Main Character–the person who the story is mostly about

Metaphor–a comparison that does *not* use the words *like* or *as;* for example, *Life is a gamble.*

Motive–the reason behind a character's action

Narrator–the person who tells the story

Nonfiction–literature which tells about real people and events